365 DAYS OF SELF-REFLECTION

365 DAYS OF SELF-REFLECTION

A year of introspection to help us grow

VINCENT PHOENIX SUMAH

Divergent Thinking Press

CONTENTS

Introduction

I often jokingly say that my studies have been my best therapy. Except that it's not a joke. Those years of studying psychosocial therapy were self-evaluations over introspections, every semester and in almost every class. So much so, that it was almost a running gag. But still, it helped me so much to understand myself, to dig deeper, to know who I was and why I did what I did.

I like to continue to reflect on who I am and understand my behaviors and ways of thinking. I like to do this in writing, it keeps my ADHD self from forgetting a large part of my thoughts. So I started looking for a "prompt book" of inner reflection.

There are a lot of "gratitude journals" or "change your life in 12 weeks" books on the market, but nothing that was to my liking. In-depth. Diversified. No magical thinking that by doing 10 minutes of meditation a day, you become happy.
And having the same question of "what am I thankful for?" every day doesn't help me develop as a human being.

But what helps me? What helps the people I work with?
Digging into our minds, into our history, into our feelings. Understanding ourselves. Demystify concepts. If we stay on the surface, the water seems dark and dense.
But if we hold our breath and dive in, we realize that rays of sunlight cross the water and show us a living and colorful world that we never thought possible.

Yes, I like analogies.

And that's what I'm offering you with this book.

No, not the analogies. Well, yes, there will be some, but I meant to dive into your ocean, one theme at a time, to discover all the beauty and life that lies beneath that frightening layer of dark water.

Everyone fills this book in their own way. You can do several questions a day and move from one topic to another. However, to do the exercise in an optimal way, I suggest answering one question per day, without skipping pages, and in the most detailed way possible.

This is an introspection book. So the goal is to elaborate on your needs, emotions and ideas. Try using as much of the lines avaiable as possible, let yourself think deeper. Add details. Write everything that comes to your mind.

Note: Throughout this book, we will refer to the ideas of *"positive"* and *"negative"*.

We define something "negative" as something **that harms us** in our daily lives or in our relationships. "Negative" **is not** something unpleasant, angry or sad. It is something that is **detrimental** to the person we want to be and the life we want to lead.

1

Gratitude

==

Gratitude journals are a dime a dozen. But after a lot of research and reading to try to include gratitude in my life (it's scientifically proven that adopting habits of gratitude is beneficial to our psychological health), I noticed that there was a little something off. I saw things like being grateful for what we have in life, seeing what we have that is beautiful instead of what we don't have or would like to have. Recognizing that what you have is already good and being happy.

I was not very comfortable with the concept.
First of all, I think it goes against the core value of humanism, which is empowerment. To be grateful for having a house, for having Netflix, for the relationship we have with people, for the mistakes of the past that made us grow, for a new book, for a campfire on a summer night... Yes, it's cool to be able to be aware that all of these things add a little bit of beauty to our lives, however, why be grateful for the things we made ourselves, by our choices?
All of these things are things that we have because of our decisions, our actions. It's like making a meal and being thankful for the meal in front

of us.

Why does this go against empowerment? By being grateful for the choices we have made, the actions we have decided to take, it erases our responsibility in all of this. Because we are grateful for what? For whom? That life has given us this? But it's not "life" that gave it to us, it's **us** who built it.

Secondly, if I trust the various gratitude quotes seen all over the internet, it encourages people to see that what they have is already beautiful, it's already enough, to take away this "pain" of always wanting more without having it.

I totally agree that not seeing the beauty we have and always focusing on what we don't have or always wanting more is not healthy.

But to be content with what you have without wanting more, should not be imposed. Some people want more out of life (could be objects, possessions, dreams or people), and telling them that they should be content with what they have makes them feel guilty for expecting more out of life.

It gives people the "I have money, a loving family, friends, I shouldn't be depressed, I have no reason to be depressed!"

It makes people think that "because they have everything they wish they had, they should be happy." It makes people feel threatened by those who want more out of life. That makes people who won't try to have more of life because they should be happy with what they have.

There are too many unhappy people, and too many people who are unhappy and don't even know it. Because it's a social condition. We're all like that, so it must be normal...

I think that incorporating gratitude into our lives is a good idea to live serenely, but we need to practice it in a way that shapes our selves to marvel at the beauty of life, and not to be "content with what we have".

So what.

What are we grateful for?

For the snow that falls in heavy flakes on a warm day. For the kind gesture a passerby offered us. The comforting taste of our favorite herbal tea (yes, we brewed it, but how cool is it that this one exists?). To be grateful is to acknowledge the beautiful.

But to do it in a healthy way, you have to recognize the beautiful in what you didn't choose or do. Like the snow falling. The blue sky. The smile of a passerby. The bird singing or the feeling of bliss as we enjoy our favorite food (as opposed to being thankful to have made/bought it).

I can be thankful that I stumbled upon the book I was looking for for a long time, compared to having a new book in general, since it was my choice to acquire it.

So let's try to see the beauty that happens in our life. Life is beautiful and there are so many things to savor and marvel at! It is time to let this beauty make its place in our days.

DATE: _____   SUBJECT: GRATITUDE

1. What are you grateful for in your life in general that you did not build yourself?

_____

_____

_____

_____

_____

_____

_____

_____

_____

_____

_____

_____

_____

_____

_____

_____

_____

_____

_____

_____

_____

_____

_____

_____

_____

_____

_____

DATE: _____ SUBJECT: GRATITUDE

2. In the space of a year, a lot can happen. Elaborate on something that was not present in your life last year, but is present today. What was your responsibility in this?

_____

_____

_____

_____

_____

_____

_____

_____

_____

_____

_____

_____

_____

_____

_____

_____

_____

_____

_____

_____

_____

_____

_____

_____

_____

_____

_____

_____

DATE: _____   SUBJECT: GRATITUDE

3. What is the best thing that happened today?

_____
_____
_____
_____
_____
_____
_____
_____
_____
_____
_____
_____
_____
_____
_____
_____
_____
_____
_____
_____
_____
_____
_____
_____
_____
_____
_____
_____
_____
_____
_____

DATE: _____   SUBJECT: GRATITUDE

4. How did you feel appreciated today?

_____
_____
_____
_____
_____
_____
_____
_____
_____
_____
_____
_____
_____
_____
_____
_____
_____
_____
_____
_____
_____
_____
_____
_____
_____
_____
_____
_____
_____
_____
_____
_____

DATE: _____   SUBJECT: GRATITUDE

5. What made you feel good today?

_____

_____

_____

_____

_____

_____

_____

_____

_____

_____

_____

_____

_____

_____

_____

_____

_____

_____

_____

_____

_____

_____

_____

_____

_____

_____

_____

DATE: _____   SUBJECT: GRATITUDE

6. Describe at least one nice thing about the weather today.

_____
_____
_____
_____
_____
_____
_____
_____
_____
_____
_____
_____
_____
_____
_____
_____
_____
_____
_____
_____
_____
_____
_____
_____
_____
_____
_____
_____

7. Were the first 6 questions easy or difficult to answer? Why or why not?

_____

_____

_____

_____

_____

_____

_____

_____

_____

_____

_____

_____

_____

_____

_____

_____

_____

_____

_____

_____

_____

_____

_____

_____

_____

_____

_____

_____

_____

DATE: _____ SUBJECT: GRATITUDE

8. What brought you joy today? This week? And this month?

_____
_____
_____
_____
_____
_____
_____
_____
_____
_____
_____
_____
_____
_____
_____
_____
_____
_____
_____
_____
_____
_____
_____
_____
_____
_____
_____
_____
_____
_____
_____
_____
_____

DATE: _____   SUBJECT: GRATITUDE

9. Tell us about a happy memory.

_____
_____
_____
_____
_____
_____
_____
_____
_____
_____
_____
_____
_____
_____
_____
_____
_____
_____
_____
_____
_____
_____
_____
_____
_____
_____
_____
_____
_____
_____
_____
_____
_____

DATE: _____   SUBJECT: GRATITUDE

10. What are the positive things (that have a beneficial impact) in your life?

_____
_____
_____
_____
_____
_____
_____
_____
_____
_____
_____
_____
_____
_____
_____
_____
_____
_____
_____
_____
_____
_____
_____
_____
_____
_____
_____
_____
_____
_____

11. What do you like about your work or studies (or your daily life, if you are not an employee or student)?

_____

_____

_____

_____

_____

_____

_____

_____

_____

_____

_____

_____

_____

_____

_____

_____

_____

_____

_____

_____

_____

_____

_____

_____

_____

_____

_____

_____

_____

12. What is your favorite smell?

_____

_____

_____

_____

_____

_____

_____

_____

_____

_____

_____

_____

_____

_____

_____

_____

_____

_____

_____

_____

_____

_____

_____

_____

_____

_____

_____

_____

_____

_____

_____

13. What things or situations usually give you joy?

_____

_____

_____

_____

_____

_____

_____

_____

_____

_____

_____

_____

_____

_____

_____

_____

_____

_____

_____

_____

_____

_____

_____

_____

_____

_____

_____

_____

_____

_____

14. What is your favorite thing you are doing lately? How does it make you feel good?

_____

_____

_____

_____

_____

_____

_____

_____

_____

_____

_____

_____

_____

_____

_____

_____

_____

_____

_____

_____

_____

_____

_____

_____

_____

_____

_____

_____

15. Name five (5) things that make you smile every time. What does this spark in you?

_____

_____

_____

_____

_____

_____

_____

_____

_____

_____

_____

_____

_____

_____

_____

_____

_____

_____

_____

_____

_____

_____

_____

_____

_____

_____

_____

_____

_____

16. What were the most pleasant moments in your memories? How do they outweigh all others?

_____

_____

_____

_____

_____

_____

_____

_____

_____

_____

_____

_____

_____

_____

_____

_____

_____

_____

_____

_____

_____

_____

_____

_____

_____

_____

_____

_____

_____

_____

_____

_____

_____

DATE: _____   SUBJECT: GRATITUDE

17. Tell about a time when you received a free act of kindness from a stranger.

_____
_____
_____
_____
_____
_____
_____
_____
_____
_____
_____
_____
_____
_____
_____
_____
_____
_____
_____
_____
_____
_____
_____
_____
_____
_____

DATE: _____   SUBJECT: GRATITUDE

18. In what ways can you be grateful for the challenges you are experiencing right now?

_____
_____
_____
_____
_____
_____
_____
_____
_____
_____
_____
_____
_____
_____
_____
_____
_____
_____
_____
_____
_____
_____
_____
_____
_____
_____
_____
_____
_____
_____
_____

DATE: _____   SUBJECT: GRATITUDE

19. What have you learned new this week that is beneficial in your life?

_____

_____

_____

_____

_____

_____

_____

_____

_____

_____

_____

_____

_____

_____

_____

_____

_____

_____

_____

_____

_____

_____

_____

_____

_____

_____

_____

_____

_____

_____

20. Who are the people you appreciate? How are they an enrichment in your life?

_____

_____

_____

_____

_____

_____

_____

_____

_____

_____

_____

_____

_____

_____

_____

_____

_____

_____

_____

_____

_____

_____

_____

_____

_____

_____

_____

_____

_____

_____

21. What opportunities have you encountered that have changed your life for the better?

_____

_____

_____

_____

_____

_____

_____

_____

_____

_____

_____

_____

_____

_____

_____

_____

_____

_____

_____

_____

_____

_____

_____

_____

_____

_____

_____

_____

_____

_____

_____

DATE: _____   SUBJECT: GRATITUDE
22. What made you laugh today?

_____
_____
_____
_____
_____
_____
_____
_____
_____
_____
_____
_____
_____
_____
_____
_____
_____
_____
_____
_____
_____
_____
_____
_____
_____
_____
_____
_____
_____
_____
_____
_____

23. What have you read or heard in the last few days that has added richness or knowledge to your life?

_____

_____

_____

_____

_____

_____

_____

_____

_____

_____

_____

_____

_____

_____

_____

_____

_____

_____

_____

_____

_____

_____

_____

_____

_____

_____

_____

_____

DATE: _____   SUBJECT: GRATITUDE

24. What was the best part of your day? Why?

_____

_____

_____

_____

_____

_____

_____

_____

_____

_____

_____

_____

_____

_____

_____

_____

_____

_____

_____

_____

_____

_____

_____

_____

_____

_____

_____

_____

_____

_____

_____

2

Here and now

==

Our thinking is constantly in the past and the future. What I said, what I have to do, what I should have done, what I should not forget, etc. When in fact, the present is the only moment over which we have full control. Who are we in the present? What does our present look like?

How has our past determined our present?

How can we become aware of the present in order to have an idea of where our future will take us?

The concept of mindfulness is to take a moment to stop time on the here and now, to become aware of what is happening right now, in our head and in our body. Apart from mindfulness meditation, let's take a portrait of who you are, here and now, at this moment in your life.

Often, we get stuck on the question, "Come on, tell me about yourself for a little bit! Who are you?"

Err I don't know... I am me? I love the outdoors and good food with friends!

Huh uh :)

What else?

Often, we think that who we are can be described by our interests, hobbies, our work and our various social roles (I'm a father of 3 - I'm married - I'm a supermarket manager - I'm athletic - I'm a gamer...)

While all of this, while important, is superficial and doesn't say that much about your uniqueness.

To dig deeper into who we are, we need to focus on our behaviors and the reasons for those behaviors (often associated with our feelings).

How well do you know yourself?

How much of what you know about yourself is really you and not social and/or family conditioning?

Let's dig in and take a global picture of you, here and now.

DATE : _____   SUBJECT : HERE & NOW

25. How do you feel when you wake up in the morning?

_____

_____

_____

_____

_____

_____

_____

_____

_____

_____

_____

_____

_____

_____

_____

_____

_____

_____

_____

_____

_____

_____

_____

_____

_____

_____

_____

_____

_____

_____

_____

_____

_____

26. What takes up the majority of your time during the day, besides work (taking care of the kids qualifies as work)/school?

_____

_____

_____

_____

_____

_____

_____

_____

_____

_____

_____

_____

_____

_____

_____

_____

_____

_____

_____

_____

_____

_____

_____

_____

_____

_____

_____

27. What is the most difficult thing to accept about yourself?

_____

_____

_____

_____

_____

_____

_____

_____

_____

_____

_____

_____

_____

_____

_____

_____

_____

_____

_____

_____

_____

_____

_____

_____

_____

_____

_____

_____

_____

_____

_____

28. What matters most to you? Why?

_____

_____

_____

_____

_____

_____

_____

_____

_____

_____

_____

_____

_____

_____

_____

_____

_____

_____

_____

_____

_____

_____

_____

_____

_____

_____

_____

_____

_____

_____

29. What makes you feel energized, refreshed and recharged?

_____

_____

_____

_____

_____

_____

_____

_____

_____

_____

_____

_____

_____

_____

_____

_____

_____

_____

_____

_____

_____

_____

_____

_____

_____

_____

_____

_____

DATE : _____   SUBJECT : HERE & NOW
30. How do you spend your free time? Why?

_____
_____
_____
_____
_____
_____
_____
_____
_____
_____
_____
_____
_____
_____
_____
_____
_____
_____
_____
_____
_____
_____
_____
_____
_____
_____
_____
_____
_____
_____

DATE : _____   SUBJECT : HERE & NOW

31. How would you like to spend your free time? Why?

_____
_____
_____
_____
_____
_____
_____
_____
_____
_____
_____
_____
_____
_____
_____
_____
_____
_____
_____
_____
_____
_____
_____
_____
_____
_____
_____
_____
_____
_____
_____
_____

32. What are you passionate about (a topic or area you're never tired of learning and/or talking about)?

_____

_____

_____

_____

_____

_____

_____

_____

_____

_____

_____

_____

_____

_____

_____

_____

_____

_____

_____

_____

_____

_____

_____

_____

_____

_____

_____

_____

33. What emotions make you feel most out of control? Describe exactly how you feel at these times.

_____

_____

_____

_____

_____

_____

_____

_____

_____

_____

_____

_____

_____

_____

_____

_____

_____

_____

_____

_____

_____

_____

_____

_____

_____

_____

_____

_____

34. What do you like best about yourself? Why?

_____

_____

_____

_____

_____

_____

_____

_____

_____

_____

_____

_____

_____

_____

_____

_____

_____

_____

_____

_____

_____

_____

_____

_____

_____

_____

_____

_____

_____

_____

35. Who is your ideal "you"?

_____
_____
_____
_____
_____
_____
_____
_____
_____
_____
_____
_____
_____
_____
_____
_____
_____
_____
_____
_____
_____
_____
_____
_____
_____
_____
_____
_____
_____
_____
_____

DATE : _____   SUBJECT : HERE & NOW

36. What makes you unique?

_____
_____
_____
_____
_____
_____
_____
_____
_____
_____
_____
_____
_____
_____
_____
_____
_____
_____
_____
_____
_____
_____
_____
_____
_____
_____
_____
_____
_____
_____

37. What is your favorite food, song, smell, activity, and person right now?

_____

_____

_____

_____

_____

_____

_____

_____

_____

_____

_____

_____

_____

_____

_____

_____

_____

_____

_____

_____

_____

_____

_____

_____

_____

_____

_____

_____

_____

38. How would you describe the relationship you have with yourself?

_____

_____

_____

_____

_____

_____

_____

_____

_____

_____

_____

_____

_____

_____

_____

_____

_____

_____

_____

_____

_____

_____

_____

_____

_____

_____

_____

_____

_____

_____

39. If you had only one year left to live, what would you spend it on? Why?

_____

_____

_____

_____

_____

_____

_____

_____

_____

_____

_____

_____

_____

_____

_____

_____

_____

_____

_____

_____

_____

_____

_____

_____

_____

_____

_____

40. Are you really doing what you want to do with your days? Do you like what you are doing with your life right now?

_____
_____
_____
_____
_____
_____
_____
_____
_____
_____
_____
_____
_____
_____
_____
_____
_____
_____
_____
_____
_____
_____
_____
_____
_____
_____
_____
_____
_____
_____

41. What are you thinking about right now? And why this specific thought?

_____

_____

_____

_____

_____

_____

_____

_____

_____

_____

_____

_____

_____

_____

_____

_____

_____

_____

_____

_____

_____

_____

_____

_____

42. Do you find that you use your time in an optimal way?

_____

_____

_____

_____

_____

_____

_____

_____

_____

_____

_____

_____

_____

_____

_____

_____

_____

_____

_____

_____

_____

_____

_____

_____

_____

_____

_____

_____

_____

43. What are your last thoughts before going to sleep?

_____

_____

_____

_____

_____

_____

_____

_____

_____

_____

_____

_____

_____

_____

_____

_____

_____

_____

_____

_____

_____

_____

_____

_____

_____

_____

_____

_____

_____

_____

_____

44. Which talent or skill you have that gives you the greatest sense of pride or satisfaction?

_____
_____
_____
_____
_____
_____
_____
_____
_____
_____
_____
_____
_____
_____
_____
_____
_____
_____
_____
_____
_____
_____
_____
_____
_____
_____
_____
_____
_____

45. Is it difficult for you to be yourself? Why or why not?

_____

_____

_____

_____

_____

_____

_____

_____

_____

_____

_____

_____

_____

_____

_____

_____

_____

_____

_____

_____

_____

_____

_____

_____

_____

_____

_____

46. What thoughts, beliefs or situations do you hang onto that no longer serve you?

_____

_____

_____

_____

_____

_____

_____

_____

_____

_____

_____

_____

_____

_____

_____

_____

_____

_____

_____

_____

_____

_____

_____

_____

_____

_____

_____

47. What have you learned lately that will lead you to a better future?

_____

_____

_____

_____

_____

_____

_____

_____

_____

_____

_____

_____

_____

_____

_____

_____

_____

_____

_____

_____

_____

_____

_____

_____

_____

_____

_____

_____

_____

_____

_____

_____

_____

48. What color would you choose to describe yourself? Why?

_____

_____

_____

_____

_____

_____

_____

_____

_____

_____

_____

_____

_____

_____

_____

_____

_____

_____

_____

_____

_____

_____

_____

_____

_____

_____

_____

_____

_____

_____

49. What clothes are you most comfortable in?

_____

_____

_____

_____

_____

_____

_____

_____

_____

_____

_____

_____

_____

_____

_____

_____

_____

_____

_____

_____

_____

_____

_____

_____

_____

_____

_____

_____

_____

50. What do you build your friendships on?

_____

_____

_____

_____

_____

_____

_____

_____

_____

_____

_____

_____

_____

_____

_____

_____

_____

_____

_____

_____

_____

_____

_____

_____

_____

_____

_____

_____

_____

51. What does "me time" look like to you?

_____

_____

_____

_____

_____

_____

_____

_____

_____

_____

_____

_____

_____

_____

_____

_____

_____

_____

_____

_____

_____

_____

_____

_____

_____

_____

_____

_____

_____

_____

_____

_____

52. Do you love the person you have become? Why or why not?

_____

_____

_____

_____

_____

_____

_____

_____

_____

_____

_____

_____

_____

_____

_____

_____

_____

_____

_____

_____

_____

_____

_____

_____

_____

_____

_____

_____

_____

_____

53. What opportunities do you currently have?

_____

_____

_____

_____

_____

_____

_____

_____

_____

_____

_____

_____

_____

_____

_____

_____

_____

_____

_____

_____

_____

_____

_____

_____

_____

_____

_____

_____

_____

_____

_____

_____

_____

_____

54. What does the word "success" mean to you?

_____

_____

_____

_____

_____

_____

_____

_____

_____

_____

_____

_____

_____

_____

_____

_____

_____

_____

_____

_____

_____

_____

_____

_____

_____

_____

_____

_____

DATE : _____   SUBJECT : HERE & NOW

55. How do you see yourself and your life in one year's time?

_____
_____
_____
_____
_____
_____
_____
_____
_____
_____
_____
_____
_____
_____
_____
_____
_____
_____
_____
_____
_____
_____
_____
_____
_____
_____
_____
_____
_____
_____
_____

3

Values

==

Values.

What are values?

What is it for?

Why is it important and how do we determine our own?

I have long wondered about the precise definition of what values are. The Collins dictionary gives us the following definition: "Moral principles and beliefs that a group think are important."

Another dictionary describe is as : "What is considered true, beautiful, good, from a personal point of view or according to the criteria of a society and which is given as an ideal to reach, as something to defend".

This is a very good start. But if we want to rephrase it so it is easier to understand concretely, a value is a rule of conduct that **we** give **to ourselves**, in **our life**.

Our values system is therefore the set of rules of conduct that we give ourselves according to what we determine to be fair to ourselves and to others. Values are the road signs of our life path. They are what determine our actions, our choices and therefore, our life.

Values are at the center of who we are as individuals and it shows in our whole being.

There are hundreds of values. From altruism to fairness, perseverance and stability. We build ourselves around these values. These values become the pillars of our "self".

And these values can be learned, chosen or imposed.

When we don't know our values, it's a bit like driving on a road and taking directions at random or according to what the person in the passenger seat tells us. The risks are there to end up getting lost or to go to another destination than the one we planned, than the one we wanted. The impact, therefore, of living according to the values of others is that we also feel psychologically lost, we do not feel where we should be in life. Lost and unstable, unbalanced, frustrated and dissatisfied.

Sometimes you think you really want to go to that destination, it's been so ingrained in you for so long. But once you get there, you don't like it, you don't feel good. And you don't understand why.

That's why it's important to do a regular exercise of rediscovering our values throughout our lives.

We see someone doing something that is none of our business, but which goes against our values, and it gets to us. There's a little fire burning inside and we have to get involved. Why do we have to get involved?

Because our values are at the center of who we are, an attack on our values, even if it's not directed at us, inevitably arouses a feeling of attack towards our whole being and that's a good part of the reason why we may react so strongly.

Because our values are our rules of conduct according to what we consider to be right, and we are not taught in life that each person is valid in their values. That values are personal. That my rules of conduct for my life are not necessarily those of others and should not be imposed on the lives of others. Because we don't all go to the same destination! Because we don't all have the same history, the same life lessons, the same priorities.

But it is still because of differences in values that people will interfere in other people's lives, gossip or insult others. It can go far, it can become very hostile.
Since most of us, growing up, are taught "good values" by our family and then by society, we think that these rules of conduct should be the rules for everyone. That if others don't follow our values, they are not good people.
But values are as personal as our favorite activities or any lifestyle that is good for us but that we are aware is not for everyone.
We can share them, but if it doesn't fit the other person, there's no problem. If the clash of values is too great, we can just decide not to hang out with that person. Just like if you meet someone with whom you have no shared interests.

So, not only is it important to know our values, but we really need to keep in mind that our values are our personal rules of conduct.
For the next few days, we are going to explore our values, discover which ones come from us, which ones are acquired, maybe even which ones were imposed on us.

Here is a non-exhaustive list of values.

Abnegation	Creativity	Growth
Abundance	Credibility	Gallantry
Acceptance	Curiosity	Generosity
Accomplishment	Commitment	Gratitude
Adaptability	Cheerfulness	Hope
Adventure	Cleanliness	Hierarchy
Affection	Care	Honesty
Altruism	Discovery	Humility
Ambition	Determination	Humor
Assiduity	Duty	Hygiene
Audacity	Devotion	Impartiality
Autonomy	Dignity	Independence
Availability	Discipline	Individuality
Bravery	Discretion	Integrity
Balance	Diversity	Introspection
Calm	Dominance	Justice
Change	Dynamism	Kindness
Charity	Elegance	Knowledge
Chastity	Empathy	Love
Civility	Encouragement	Leadership
Coherence	Endurance	Non-violence
Community	Ethics	Originality
Compassion	Excellence	Open-mindedness
Compliance	Enjoyment	Perseverance
Comfort	Friendship	Professionalism
Contribution	Family	Power
Control	Firmness	Respect
Conviviality	Flexibility	Simplicity
Cooperation	Faith	Teamwork
Courtesy	Freedom	Wisdom

56. What are your 5 most important values (rules of conduct) in your life? Why are they important?

_____
_____
_____
_____
_____
_____
_____
_____
_____
_____
_____
_____
_____
_____
_____
_____
_____
_____
_____
_____
_____
_____
_____
_____
_____
_____
_____
_____
_____

DATE: _____   SUBJECT: VALUES

57. What are "good values" for you?

_____
_____
_____
_____
_____
_____
_____
_____
_____
_____
_____
_____
_____
_____
_____
_____
_____
_____
_____
_____
_____
_____
_____
_____
_____
_____
_____
_____
_____

58. Of the 5 values identified earlier, try to define your "top 3". Why did you identify these three in particular?

_____

_____

_____

_____

_____

_____

_____

_____

_____

_____

_____

_____

_____

_____

_____

_____

_____

_____

_____

_____

_____

_____

_____

_____

_____

_____

59. If someone has different values (not the same top 5 as you), what does that tell you about that person?

_____

_____

_____

_____

_____

_____

_____

_____

_____

_____

_____

_____

_____

_____

_____

_____

_____

_____

_____

_____

_____

_____

_____

_____

_____

_____

_____

60. Are you the kind of person you would be friends with? Why?

_____

_____

_____

_____

_____

_____

_____

_____

_____

_____

_____

_____

_____

_____

_____

_____

_____

_____

_____

_____

_____

_____

_____

_____

_____

_____

_____

61. What qualities do you most admire in people?

_____

_____

_____

_____

_____

_____

_____

_____

_____

_____

_____

_____

_____

_____

_____

_____

_____

_____

_____

_____

_____

_____

_____

_____

_____

_____

_____

_____

62. What battle (figurative) could you let go of? Why haven't you already done so? What would you need?

_____

_____

_____

_____

_____

_____

_____

_____

_____

_____

_____

_____

_____

_____

_____

_____

_____

_____

_____

_____

_____

_____

_____

_____

_____

_____

63. What battle would you never want to give up? Why? What do you gain from this battle?

_____

_____

_____

_____

_____

_____

_____

_____

_____

_____

_____

_____

_____

_____

_____

_____

_____

_____

_____

_____

_____

_____

_____

_____

_____

_____

_____

_____

64. What values do you associate with friendship? For each one, explain why it is important to you.

_____
_____
_____
_____
_____
_____
_____
_____
_____
_____
_____
_____
_____
_____
_____
_____
_____
_____
_____
_____
_____
_____
_____
_____
_____
_____

DATE: _____

65. Who is the person you value most?

_____

_____

_____

_____

_____

_____

_____

_____

_____

_____

_____

_____

_____

_____

_____

_____

_____

_____

_____

_____

_____

_____

_____

_____

_____

_____

_____

DATE: _____   SUBJECT: VALUES

66. On what subject/situation/behavior do you categorically refuse to compromise?

_____
_____
_____
_____
_____
_____
_____
_____
_____
_____
_____
_____
_____
_____
_____
_____
_____
_____
_____
_____
_____
_____
_____
_____
_____

67. What makes you feel empowered or proud?

_____

_____

_____

_____

_____

_____

_____

_____

_____

_____

_____

_____

_____

_____

_____

_____

_____

_____

_____

_____

_____

_____

_____

_____

_____

_____

_____

_____

_____

_____

68. What exasperates you in others (as a behavior or way of life)? Why?

_____

_____

_____

_____

_____

_____

_____

_____

_____

_____

_____

_____

_____

_____

_____

_____

_____

_____

_____

_____

_____

_____

_____

_____

_____

_____

_____

_____

_____

_____

_____

_____

69. What are the values of the politicians or political parties you vote for?

_____

_____

_____

_____

_____

_____

_____

_____

_____

_____

_____

_____

_____

_____

_____

_____

_____

_____

_____

_____

_____

_____

_____

_____

_____

70. What makes you angry or irritated for sure? Why?

_____

_____

_____

_____

_____

_____

_____

_____

_____

_____

_____

_____

_____

_____

_____

_____

_____

_____

_____

_____

_____

_____

_____

_____

_____

_____

_____

_____

_____

71. What makes you proud of the accomplishments or behaviors of your family members?

_____

_____

_____

_____

_____

_____

_____

_____

_____

_____

_____

_____

_____

_____

_____

_____

_____

_____

_____

_____

_____

_____

_____

_____

_____

_____

_____

DATE: _____   SUBJECT: VALUES

72. What thing/everyday situation would you miss the most if it were taken away?

_____
_____
_____
_____
_____
_____
_____
_____
_____
_____
_____
_____
_____
_____
_____
_____
_____
_____
_____
_____
_____
_____
_____
_____
_____

73. When you are not working/studying/taking care of the kids, what do you use most of your time on?

_____
_____
_____
_____
_____
_____
_____
_____
_____
_____
_____
_____
_____
_____
_____
_____
_____
_____
_____
_____
_____
_____
_____
_____
_____
_____
_____

74. Who do you admire the most? Why?

_____
_____
_____
_____
_____
_____
_____
_____
_____
_____
_____
_____
_____
_____
_____
_____
_____
_____
_____
_____
_____
_____
_____
_____
_____
_____
_____
_____
_____

75. What topics are you told you overreact about?

_____

_____

_____

_____

_____

_____

_____

_____

_____

_____

_____

_____

_____

_____

_____

_____

_____

_____

_____

_____

_____

_____

_____

_____

_____

_____

_____

_____

76. What have you learned about your values from the last 20 questions?

_____

_____

_____

_____

_____

_____

_____

_____

_____

_____

_____

_____

_____

_____

_____

_____

_____

_____

_____

_____

_____

_____

_____

_____

_____

_____

_____

_____

_____

_____

4

Spheres of Life

===

Life is a recipe of about 14 ingredients.

To make our life taste good, we need to put a bit of these 14 ingredients on our plate.

What happens too often in our capitalist society is that we are pushed and trained to put only a few ingredients in our dish : family, work/study, money and sometimes friends. Because we have to make money for companies. No time to have a balanced life, time is money! Here are a few ingredients, be happy with them.

We often take the liberty of adding leisure and hobbies to our plate, but even with 5 ingredients out of 14, it is normal that in the long run our life seems bland. And it is also normal that if we remove one of our few ingredients, the difference is noticeable. We may react strongly because that's all we have to feed us.

But when our life is full of ingredients, full of different tastes, not only can we start to play with flavors, but we are able to find alternatives when we are missing an ingredient to cook something tasty anyway!

In a less analogical language, life is divided into more or less 14 spheres. Each of these spheres is important to maintain good physical and psychological health, but we only give importance to some of them. We have the impression that we can't "enjoy life" because of all the time and energy we give to these few spheres (family, work/studies).

Not only do we need to be aware of the other spheres and give them some love as well, but we also need to reflect on our overall satisfaction with each of these spheres: Friends & Family, Love & Sexuality, Personal Goals, Pleasures & Hobbies, Physical Environment, Finances, Career & Education, Physical Health, Psychological Health, Spirituality & Personal Growth, Creativity & Intellectual Stimulation, Self Esteem & Personal Image, Connection to the World & Community and Contribution to the World.

Because if we only give attention to a few things, but we are not satisfied with them, it is normal that life seems grey and bland.

Let's take the time to make a global introspection of our spheres of life and our level of satisfaction.

77. Tell us about a time when you felt betrayed by a friend. Why did you feel betrayed? What did this tell you about the friend? Why did it happen?

_____

_____

_____

_____

_____

_____

_____

_____

_____

_____

_____

_____

_____

_____

_____

_____

_____

_____

_____

_____

_____

_____

_____

_____

_____

_____

_____

78. What difficulties do you encounter in your friendships?

79. How important is family (your parents, siblings, aunts/uncles, etc.) in your life? Why?

_____

_____

_____

_____

_____

_____

_____

_____

_____

_____

_____

_____

_____

_____

_____

_____

_____

_____

_____

_____

_____

_____

_____

_____

_____

_____

_____

80. What expectations do you have of your family? Are they aware of these expectations?

_____

_____

_____

_____

_____

_____

_____

_____

_____

_____

_____

_____

_____

_____

_____

_____

_____

_____

_____

_____

_____

_____

_____

_____

_____

_____

_____

_____

81. What difficulties do you experience with your family members? How do you have control over possible solutions?

_____

_____

_____

_____

_____

_____

_____

_____

_____

_____

_____

_____

_____

_____

_____

_____

_____

_____

_____

_____

_____

_____

_____

_____

_____

_____

82. What impact (positive and/or negative) do your relationships with family members have on your psychological health?

_____

_____

_____

_____

_____

_____

_____

_____

_____

_____

_____

_____

_____

_____

_____

_____

_____

_____

_____

_____

_____

_____

_____

_____

_____

_____

83. Is your love life currently satisfying? Why?

84. Is there anything that could be added/changed to your love life in the next few days or weeks to make it more satisfying?

_____

_____

_____

_____

_____

_____

_____

_____

_____

_____

_____

_____

_____

_____

_____

_____

_____

_____

_____

_____

_____

_____

_____

_____

_____

_____

85. What did you learn from your most recent break-up? Are there any psychological or physical scars?

_____

_____

_____

_____

_____

_____

_____

_____

_____

_____

_____

_____

_____

_____

_____

_____

_____

_____

_____

_____

_____

_____

_____

_____

_____

_____

86. What is necessary to have in a romantic relationship for it to be satisfying and meaningful?

_____

_____

_____

_____

_____

_____

_____

_____

_____

_____

_____

_____

_____

_____

_____

_____

_____

_____

_____

_____

_____

_____

_____

_____

_____

_____

_____

_____

87. What are your expectations of your romantic partners? Are these expectations verbalized? Why?

_____

_____

_____

_____

_____

_____

_____

_____

_____

_____

_____

_____

_____

_____

_____

_____

_____

_____

_____

_____

_____

_____

_____

_____

_____

_____

_____

88. How do you prefer to be loved and cared for?

_____

_____

_____

_____

_____

_____

_____

_____

_____

_____

_____

_____

_____

_____

_____

_____

_____

_____

_____

_____

_____

_____

_____

_____

_____

_____

_____

_____

_____

_____

89. What does sexuality (alone or with someone else) mean to you? What role does sexuality play in your love life?

_____

_____

_____

_____

_____

_____

_____

_____

_____

_____

_____

_____

_____

_____

_____

_____

_____

_____

_____

_____

_____

_____

_____

_____

_____

_____

_____

_____

_____

DATE: _____   SUBJECT: SPHERES OF LIFE

90. Do you consider your sex life to be satisfying? Why?

_____

_____

_____

_____

_____

_____

_____

_____

_____

_____

_____

_____

_____

_____

_____

_____

_____

_____

_____

_____

_____

_____

_____

_____

_____

_____

_____

_____

_____

_____

91. What could and/or should be changed in your sex life for greater satisfaction?

_____

_____

_____

_____

_____

_____

_____

_____

_____

_____

_____

_____

_____

_____

_____

_____

_____

_____

_____

_____

_____

_____

_____

_____

_____

_____

92. Do you feel respected by your partners in your sexuality? Why? If now, what could you do to address this?

_____

_____

_____

_____

_____

_____

_____

_____

_____

_____

_____

_____

_____

_____

_____

_____

_____

_____

_____

_____

_____

_____

_____

_____

_____

_____

_____

DATE: _____   SUBJECT: SPHERES OF LIFE

93. Outside of school and work, what are your personal goals for your life? What would you like to accomplish or acquire in your life? Name 20, no matter how small these goals are.

_____

_____

_____

_____

_____

_____

_____

_____

_____

_____

_____

_____

_____

_____

_____

_____

_____

_____

_____

_____

_____

_____

_____

_____

_____

_____

_____

94. Is it important for you to have personal goals (not related to your work or family)? Why?

_____

_____

_____

_____

_____

_____

_____

_____

_____

_____

_____

_____

_____

_____

_____

_____

_____

_____

_____

_____

_____

_____

_____

_____

_____

_____

_____

95. How do you feel when you have just accomplished a project or goal?

_____

_____

_____

_____

_____

_____

_____

_____

_____

_____

_____

_____

_____

_____

_____

_____

_____

_____

_____

_____

_____

_____

_____

_____

_____

96. What dream would you like to achieve, whether it is realistic or not? How is it realistic or unrealistic?

_____

_____

_____

_____

_____

_____

_____

_____

_____

_____

_____

_____

_____

_____

_____

_____

_____

_____

_____

_____

_____

_____

_____

_____

_____

_____

_____

_____

97. In relation to this dream, what are the steps (in any order and no matter how small) that need to be accomplished and the items that need to be acquired? What can you start this week?

_____

_____

_____

_____

_____

_____

_____

_____

_____

_____

_____

_____

_____

_____

_____

_____

_____

_____

_____

_____

_____

_____

_____

_____

_____

98. If you have dreams and aspirations that you describe as "unrealistic," how could that dream be modified to make it more realistic? What could you do to get a little closer to it?

_____

_____

_____

_____

_____

_____

_____

_____

_____

_____

_____

_____

_____

_____

_____

_____

_____

_____

_____

_____

_____

_____

_____

_____

_____

_____

_____

_____

99. What are your hobbies? Your interests? Activities just for you?

_____

_____

_____

_____

_____

_____

_____

_____

_____

_____

_____

_____

_____

_____

_____

_____

_____

_____

_____

_____

_____

_____

_____

_____

_____

_____

_____

_____

_____

100. What new hobbies and interests have you incorporated into your life in the past year? Were they new discoveries? How do you feel about this?

_____

_____

_____

_____

_____

_____

_____

_____

_____

_____

_____

_____

_____

_____

_____

_____

_____

_____

_____

_____

_____

_____

_____

_____

_____

_____

_____

101. Think about your favorite hobby. How does it re-energize you?

_____

_____

_____

_____

_____

_____

_____

_____

_____

_____

_____

_____

_____

_____

_____

_____

_____

_____

_____

_____

_____

_____

_____

_____

_____

_____

_____

_____

_____

_____

_____

_____

102. Do you ever feel guilty about taking time for your hobbies? If so, why? If not, did this ever happen to you?

_____

_____

_____

_____

_____

_____

_____

_____

_____

_____

_____

_____

_____

_____

_____

_____

_____

_____

_____

_____

_____

_____

_____

_____

_____

_____

103. Approximately how much time per week do you give to your interests, hobbies, activities just for you? Is this enough for you? How much control do you have in this situation?

_____

_____

_____

_____

_____

_____

_____

_____

_____

_____

_____

_____

_____

_____

_____

_____

_____

_____

_____

_____

_____

_____

_____

_____

_____

104. What new activities or hobbies would you like to try/master if there were no limitations?

_____

_____

_____

_____

_____

_____

_____

_____

_____

_____

_____

_____

_____

_____

_____

_____

_____

_____

_____

_____

_____

_____

_____

_____

_____

_____

_____

_____

_____

105. Do you like where you live? The city, the neighborhood, the house/apartment? Why or why not? What do you like best? What could be improved?

_____

_____

_____

_____

_____

_____

_____

_____

_____

_____

_____

_____

_____

_____

_____

_____

_____

_____

_____

_____

_____

_____

_____

_____

106. Why did you choose to live in this specific place?

_____

_____

_____

_____

_____

_____

_____

_____

_____

_____

_____

_____

_____

_____

_____

_____

_____

_____

_____

_____

_____

_____

_____

_____

_____

_____

_____

_____

_____

_____

107. What is the room in your home where you feel most comfortable? Why?

_____

_____

_____

_____

_____

_____

_____

_____

_____

_____

_____

_____

_____

_____

_____

_____

_____

_____

_____

_____

_____

_____

_____

_____

_____

_____

_____

108. What area of your home could be improved to make you feel better?

_____

_____

_____

_____

_____

_____

_____

_____

_____

_____

_____

_____

_____

_____

_____

_____

_____

_____

_____

_____

_____

_____

_____

_____

_____

109. After a day of school or work, how do you feel about coming home?

_____

_____

_____

_____

_____

_____

_____

_____

_____

_____

_____

_____

_____

_____

_____

_____

_____

_____

_____

_____

_____

_____

_____

_____

_____

_____

_____

110. How do you feel about your bank account? Is your financial situation satisfying to you?

_____

_____

_____

_____

_____

_____

_____

_____

_____

_____

_____

_____

_____

_____

_____

_____

_____

_____

_____

_____

_____

_____

_____

_____

_____

_____

111. Where does your monthly income come from (salary/child support/government/etc.). Can it be cut off overnight? Is this a stress factor?

_____

_____

_____

_____

_____

_____

_____

_____

_____

_____

_____

_____

_____

_____

_____

_____

_____

_____

_____

_____

_____

_____

_____

_____

_____

_____

_____

112. Do you have any money saved up? If you were to lose your (or one of your) incomes, how long could you live on your savings? How does that make you feel? What could you do to improve the situation?

_____

_____

_____

_____

_____

_____

_____

_____

_____

_____

_____

_____

_____

_____

_____

_____

_____

_____

_____

_____

_____

_____

_____

_____

_____

_____

113. Is money a stress factor for you? Why or why not? What choices could you make to be more at peace with your financial sphere? What does this imply?

_____

_____

_____

_____

_____

_____

_____

_____

_____

_____

_____

_____

_____

_____

_____

_____

_____

_____

_____

_____

_____

_____

_____

_____

_____

DATE: _____   SUBJECT: SPHERES OF LIFE

114. Other than your rent and food, where does most of your monthly income go? Why?

_____

_____

_____

_____

_____

_____

_____

_____

_____

_____

_____

_____

_____

_____

_____

_____

_____

_____

_____

_____

_____

_____

_____

_____

_____

_____

DATE: _____   SUBJECT: SPHERES OF LIFE

115. Why did you choose this field of study/work?

_____
_____
_____
_____
_____
_____
_____
_____
_____
_____
_____
_____
_____
_____
_____
_____
_____
_____
_____
_____
_____
_____
_____
_____
_____
_____
_____
_____
_____
_____
_____

116. What did you want to do when you were a child? Has it changed? Why or why not?

_____

_____

_____

_____

_____

_____

_____

_____

_____

_____

_____

_____

_____

_____

_____

_____

_____

_____

_____

_____

_____

_____

_____

_____

_____

_____

_____

_____

_____

117. What are the good and bad things about your work/study environment? If you are neither working nor studying, what are the good and bad aspects of your daily environment?

_____

_____

_____

_____

_____

_____

_____

_____

_____

_____

_____

_____

_____

_____

_____

_____

_____

_____

_____

_____

_____

_____

_____

_____

_____

118. In relation to these bad aspects, can they be modified to be more satisfying? How or why not?

_____
_____
_____
_____
_____
_____
_____
_____
_____
_____
_____
_____
_____
_____
_____
_____
_____
_____
_____
_____
_____
_____
_____
_____
_____
_____
_____
_____
_____
_____

119. If you could do anything as a career overnight and make a decent living, what would it be? Why?

_____

_____

_____

_____

_____

_____

_____

_____

_____

_____

_____

_____

_____

_____

_____

_____

_____

_____

_____

_____

_____

_____

_____

_____

_____

_____

_____

_____

120. How do you feel in your body, physically (pain, ease of movement, appearance, etc.)?

_____

_____

_____

_____

_____

_____

_____

_____

_____

_____

_____

_____

_____

_____

_____

_____

_____

_____

_____

_____

_____

_____

_____

_____

_____

_____

_____

121. Do you engage in any physical activity? If yes, which one and why?
If not, why not?

_____

_____

_____

_____

_____

_____

_____

_____

_____

_____

_____

_____

_____

_____

_____

_____

_____

_____

_____

_____

_____

_____

_____

_____

_____

_____

_____

_____

122. Are you satisfied with your physical health? Why or why not?

_____

_____

_____

_____

_____

_____

_____

_____

_____

_____

_____

_____

_____

_____

_____

_____

_____

_____

_____

_____

_____

_____

_____

_____

_____

_____

_____

_____

_____

_____

123. Do you have any physical health problems? If so, what are they? Are you at peace with your diagnoses?

_____

_____

_____

_____

_____

_____

_____

_____

_____

_____

_____

_____

_____

_____

_____

_____

_____

_____

_____

_____

_____

_____

_____

_____

_____

_____

124. What is the unhealthiest food you like to eat? Why do you still eat it?

_____

_____

_____

_____

_____

_____

_____

_____

_____

_____

_____

_____

_____

_____

_____

_____

_____

_____

_____

_____

_____

_____

_____

_____

_____

_____

_____

DATE: _____   SUBJECT: SPHERES OF LIFE

125. Do you have trouble falling asleep at night? If so, what keeps you awake? Also, describe what the 2 hours before you go to bed are like?

_____
_____
_____
_____
_____
_____
_____
_____
_____
_____
_____
_____
_____
_____
_____
_____
_____
_____
_____
_____
_____
_____
_____
_____
_____
_____
_____
_____
_____

DATE: _____   SUBJECT: SPHERES OF LIFE

126. As precisely as possible, what is it that stresses you in life? What actions can you take to face it?

_____
_____
_____
_____
_____
_____
_____
_____
_____
_____
_____
_____
_____
_____
_____
_____
_____
_____
_____
_____
_____
_____
_____
_____
_____
_____
_____
_____
_____

127. Under what circumstances do you imagine worst-case scenarios?
What are your irrational fears?

_____

_____

_____

_____

_____

_____

_____

_____

_____

_____

_____

_____

_____

_____

_____

_____

_____

_____

_____

_____

_____

_____

_____

_____

_____

_____

_____

_____

128. Do you feel validated and encouraged by those around you? In what ways?

_____

_____

_____

_____

_____

_____

_____

_____

_____

_____

_____

_____

_____

_____

_____

_____

_____

_____

_____

_____

_____

_____

_____

_____

_____

_____

_____

_____

_____

_____

129. Do you feel that you are in control of your life, your choices, your decisions? Why or why not?

_____

_____

_____

_____

_____

_____

_____

_____

_____

_____

_____

_____

_____

_____

_____

_____

_____

_____

_____

_____

_____

_____

_____

_____

_____

_____

_____

_____

130. What is the meaning you have decided to give to your life? Why?

_____

_____

_____

_____

_____

_____

_____

_____

_____

_____

_____

_____

_____

_____

_____

_____

_____

_____

_____

_____

_____

_____

_____

_____

_____

_____

_____

_____

_____

_____

131. Are you spiritual? Do you have any spiritual or religious beliefs? If so, what are they and what do they bring you? If not, why not? Is it something you miss?

_____

_____

_____

_____

_____

_____

_____

_____

_____

_____

_____

_____

_____

_____

_____

_____

_____

_____

_____

_____

_____

_____

_____

_____

132. Think about yourself 5 years ago. How have you improved as a person? What still needs to be improved?

_____

_____

_____

_____

_____

_____

_____

_____

_____

_____

_____

_____

_____

_____

_____

_____

_____

_____

_____

_____

_____

_____

_____

_____

_____

_____

_____

_____

_____

_____

133. What degree of zenitude would you like to achieve in the course of your life? Give examples if possible.

_____

_____

_____

_____

_____

_____

_____

_____

_____

_____

_____

_____

_____

_____

_____

_____

_____

_____

_____

_____

_____

_____

_____

_____

_____

_____

_____

_____

_____

_____

_____

134. What stimulates you intellectually?

_____

_____

_____

_____

_____

_____

_____

_____

_____

_____

_____

_____

_____

_____

_____

_____

_____

_____

_____

_____

_____

_____

_____

_____

_____

_____

_____

135. What do you like to create (art, food, technology, etc.) What do you wish you could create?

_____

_____

_____

_____

_____

_____

_____

_____

_____

_____

_____

_____

_____

_____

_____

_____

_____

_____

_____

_____

_____

_____

_____

_____

136. What are your favorite topics of conversation (those that keep you talking for hours)?

_____

_____

_____

_____

_____

_____

_____

_____

_____

_____

_____

_____

_____

_____

_____

_____

_____

_____

_____

_____

_____

_____

_____

_____

_____

_____

_____

_____

137. How is your self-esteem? Are you the kind of person you would like to have as a friend? Why or why not?

_____

_____

_____

_____

_____

_____

_____

_____

_____

_____

_____

_____

_____

_____

_____

_____

_____

_____

_____

_____

_____

_____

_____

_____

_____

_____

138. Does it matter to you what others think about you? Why or why not?

_____

_____

_____

_____

_____

_____

_____

_____

_____

_____

_____

_____

_____

_____

_____

_____

_____

_____

_____

_____

_____

_____

_____

_____

_____

_____

_____

_____

139. What would you like people to say about you? Why?

_____

_____

_____

_____

_____

_____

_____

_____

_____

_____

_____

_____

_____

_____

_____

_____

_____

_____

_____

_____

_____

_____

_____

_____

_____

_____

_____

_____

_____

_____

_____

_____

_____

140. What does it mean to you to be confident?

141. Do you belong to a group or community (whether it's about a nationality, a passion, an identity, etc.). If not, why? And if so, do you have a sense of belonging with your communities?

_____
_____
_____
_____
_____
_____
_____
_____
_____
_____
_____
_____
_____
_____
_____
_____
_____
_____
_____
_____
_____
_____
_____
_____
_____
_____
_____
_____

142. Describe your neighborhood life. What do you like, what do you dislike?

_____

_____

_____

_____

_____

_____

_____

_____

_____

_____

_____

_____

_____

_____

_____

_____

_____

_____

_____

_____

_____

_____

_____

_____

_____

_____

_____

_____

143. What would you like to leave to the world or your community in your life? How would you like to make a difference?

_____

_____

_____

_____

_____

_____

_____

_____

_____

_____

_____

_____

_____

_____

_____

_____

_____

_____

_____

_____

_____

_____

_____

_____

_____

_____

_____

_____

_____

_____

_____

144. Is connecting with the world, different cultures, people, etc. important to you? Why or why not?

_____

_____

_____

_____

_____

_____

_____

_____

_____

_____

_____

_____

_____

_____

_____

_____

_____

_____

_____

_____

_____

_____

_____

_____

_____

_____

_____

_____

_____

_____

5

Procrastination &
Execution

*"Things are not difficult to make;
what is difficult is putting ourselves in the
state of mind to make them."*
—— **Constantin Brancusi**

==

Procrastination. Putting off our tasks for later. It's a big problem for many people. But why do we procrastinate? We KNOW we have to do our chores, we have to study, we have laundry or food to do. The short answer is that our emotional sphere speaks very loudly. "We don't feel like" doing our chores, studying, doing our laundry. It's boring, it takes effort, energy, we'd like to do something else more challenging or fun, or we're afraid of the outcome, etc.
The long answer is that there are many possible reasons that cause procrastination and difficulty in getting things done and each of these reasons requires a different approach.

What we hear most often, however, is : I don't have the motivation. But actually, that's not always true. We have the motivation. Motivation is the reason why we want or know that we have to do our tasks, our study, our laundry, etc.,

Because it's our job. Motivation.
Because we want to get our degree. Motivation.
Because we're going to need clean laundry. Motivation.
I'm hungry, so I make food. Hunger is my motivation, my reason, for making food. Whether or not I get up to make food for myself is another story. It can be a matter of execution, sometimes of fatigue, fear or something else.

What is wrongly called "motivation" is actually "executive energy", "action energy". It is in the execution, in the mobilization and sometimes in the self-discipline that there is a problem and it is precisely because we have a very clear motivation that we tend to feel guilty about the lack of execution. We WANT to do it most of the time (not in the sense that we are always interested in doing it, but that we know we should) and we know why we want to do it. But we don't do it.

Before jumping into the solution avenues, we need to take the time to ask ourselves questions to find out why we procrastinate.

SUBJECT : PROCRASTINATION & EXECUTION

DATE: _____

145. When you know you need to do something now and you don't do it, why? What thoughts are going on inside you that are preventing you from taking action?

_____
_____
_____
_____
_____
_____
_____
_____
_____
_____
_____
_____
_____
_____
_____
_____
_____
_____
_____
_____
_____
_____
_____
_____

DATE: _____

146. Are there any positive aspects to procrastination (i.e., putting something off) and if so, what are they?

_____

_____

_____

_____

_____

_____

_____

_____

_____

_____

_____

_____

_____

_____

_____

_____

_____

_____

_____

_____

_____

_____

_____

_____

_____

_____

_____

DATE: _____

147. What do you do when you procrastinate, instead of doing your tasks?

_____
_____
_____
_____
_____
_____
_____
_____
_____
_____
_____
_____
_____
_____
_____
_____
_____
_____
_____
_____
_____
_____
_____
_____
_____
_____
_____
_____

DATE: _____

148. For which tasks are you most likely to procrastinate? Why?

_____
_____
_____
_____
_____
_____
_____
_____
_____
_____
_____
_____
_____
_____
_____
_____
_____
_____
_____
_____
_____
_____
_____
_____
_____
_____
_____
_____

SUBJECT : PROCRASTINATION & EXECUTION

DATE: _____

149. What did you procrastinate on today? Why? How long would it have taken you to do this task?

_____
_____
_____
_____
_____
_____
_____
_____
_____
_____
_____
_____
_____
_____
_____
_____
_____
_____
_____
_____
_____
_____
_____
_____
_____
_____
_____

SUBJECT : PROCRASTINATION & EXECUTION
DATE: _____

150. What is the most difficult thing about execution/action? Why is that?

_____
_____
_____
_____
_____
_____
_____
_____
_____
_____
_____
_____
_____
_____
_____
_____
_____
_____
_____
_____
_____
_____
_____
_____
_____
_____
_____
_____

SUBJECT : PROCRASTINATION & EXECUTION

DATE: _____

151. What do you think you need to take action? What is missing?

_____

_____

_____

_____

_____

_____

_____

_____

_____

_____

_____

_____

_____

_____

_____

_____

_____

_____

_____

_____

_____

_____

_____

_____

_____

_____

_____

_____

_____

_____

_____

_____

_____

SUBJECT : PROCRASTINATION & EXECUTION
DATE: _____
152. For this week, what 3 actions are you willing to commit to that will bring you closer to your goals?

_____

_____

_____

_____

_____

_____

_____

_____

_____

_____

_____

_____

_____

_____

_____

_____

_____

_____

_____

_____

_____

_____

_____

_____

_____

_____

_____

DATE: _____

153. Have you ever yelled at someone or been very angry because they didn't do something?

_____
_____
_____
_____
_____
_____
_____
_____
_____
_____
_____
_____
_____
_____
_____
_____
_____
_____
_____
_____
_____
_____
_____
_____
_____
_____
_____

154. Do you know anyone who seems to be always "motivated" or "in action"? How do you feel about this? How do you think they do it?

_____

_____

_____

_____

_____

_____

_____

_____

_____

_____

_____

_____

_____

_____

_____

_____

_____

_____

_____

_____

_____

_____

_____

_____

_____

_____

155. Do you tend to belittle/blame/guilt yourself when you procrastinate? Why or why not? What do you tell yourself?

_____

_____

_____

_____

_____

_____

_____

_____

_____

_____

_____

_____

_____

_____

_____

_____

_____

_____

_____

_____

_____

_____

_____

_____

_____

SUBJECT : PROCRASTINATION & EXECUTION
DATE: _____

156. What do you think about laziness? Do you find yourself lazy? Why?

157. And if we say that laziness does not exist, what could be the reasons that prevent us from taking action?

_____

_____

_____

_____

_____

_____

_____

_____

_____

_____

_____

_____

_____

_____

_____

_____

_____

_____

_____

_____

_____

_____

_____

_____

_____

_____

158. Are you the type of person who hesitates to take action if the context/situation is not perfect (e.g., having enough money, enough energy, being in a hurry, etc.) Why do you think that is?

_____

_____

_____

_____

_____

_____

_____

_____

_____

_____

_____

_____

_____

_____

_____

_____

_____

_____

_____

_____

_____

_____

_____

_____

_____

_____

_____

159. When faced with a task, can you easily determine the steps to take to complete that task (even if it's just doing the dishes)?

_____

_____

_____

_____

_____

_____

_____

_____

_____

_____

_____

_____

_____

_____

_____

_____

_____

_____

_____

_____

_____

_____

_____

_____

_____

DATE: _____

160. Do you have trouble making decisions? Are you afraid of making a bad decision? Do you feel that it is a barrier to action?

_____

_____

_____

_____

_____

_____

_____

_____

_____

_____

_____

_____

_____

_____

_____

_____

_____

_____

_____

_____

_____

_____

_____

_____

_____

_____

SUBJECT : PROCRASTINATION & EXECUTION

DATE: _____

161. With the reflection of the questions in this topic, what did you discover about yourself and your procrastination? What could you implement to procrastinate less?

_____
_____
_____
_____
_____
_____
_____
_____
_____
_____
_____
_____
_____
_____
_____
_____
_____
_____
_____
_____
_____
_____
_____
_____
_____

6

Fears

"Fear is the path to the dark side.
Fear leads to anger.
Anger leads to hate.
Hate leads to suffering."
—— **Yoda**

===

Fear.
It paralyzes our body as well as our mind and creates a lot of feelings that are not always pleasant to live with, such as anxiety or the feeling of being inadequate.

Fear makes us wary of possible danger.
Fear makes us hostile to what we don't understand, because in what we don't understand, there is the risk of danger.

But fear is normal and is part of our survival instinct. Without fear, we would never escape from danger. Even though we live in a modern and rather safe world, our brain is still doing one of its basic functions : scanning everything around us and everything that happens to detect danger. And because it struggles to find them, it often decides that the interview we are about to have is a danger. That the person who lives differently from us is a danger. That not making "the right choices" is a danger. That not being perfect in our tasks is a danger. And it reacts to these dangers in the same way that it reacts to a real danger to our physical safety.

Sometimes our fears convince us that we are in danger so much that we let our survival instinct take control of us. And if this is indeed effective in front of a mammoth, it is much less effective in a social or everyday situation.

But even if stress and fears are normal, they can still become an obstacle to our progress and fulfillment when we let our fears take control.

Trying to understand more about our fears allows us to have a more global vision of how our brain works, what we fear, and allows us to establish adapted solutions.

DATE: _____   SUBJECT: FEAR

162. What do you think fear is? Why do we experience fear?

_____

_____

_____

_____

_____

_____

_____

_____

_____

_____

_____

_____

_____

_____

_____

_____

_____

_____

_____

_____

_____

_____

_____

_____

_____

_____

_____

163. What are your biggest, most obvious fears? What other fears lie beneath them?

_____

_____

_____

_____

_____

_____

_____

_____

_____

_____

_____

_____

_____

_____

_____

_____

_____

_____

_____

_____

_____

_____

_____

_____

_____

_____

_____

164. What triggers anxiety (fear of a hypothetical situation) without fail?

_____

_____

_____

_____

_____

_____

_____

_____

_____

_____

_____

_____

_____

_____

_____

_____

_____

_____

_____

_____

_____

_____

_____

_____

_____

_____

_____

165. is there something in your life that you really want to do, or a certain passion/dream that you have, but are not doing because you are afraid? What is it and what are you afraid of?

_____

_____

_____

_____

_____

_____

_____

_____

_____

_____

_____

_____

_____

_____

_____

_____

_____

_____

_____

_____

_____

_____

_____

_____

_____

_____

166. What topics make you uncomfortable to talk about? Why?

_____

_____

_____

_____

_____

_____

_____

_____

_____

_____

_____

_____

_____

_____

_____

_____

_____

_____

_____

_____

_____

_____

_____

_____

_____

_____

_____

_____

_____

_____

_____

167. What worries you about the future? Why?

_____

_____

_____

_____

_____

_____

_____

_____

_____

_____

_____

_____

_____

_____

_____

_____

_____

_____

_____

_____

_____

_____

_____

_____

_____

_____

_____

_____

_____

_____

168. Do you feel anxious about others judging you? Why or why not?

_____

_____

_____

_____

_____

_____

_____

_____

_____

_____

_____

_____

_____

_____

_____

_____

_____

_____

_____

_____

_____

_____

_____

_____

_____

_____

_____

_____

_____

DATE: _____   SUBJECT: FEAR

169. What would you do in the next month if you had no fear?

_____
_____
_____
_____
_____
_____
_____
_____
_____
_____
_____
_____
_____
_____
_____
_____
_____
_____
_____
_____
_____
_____
_____
_____
_____
_____
_____
_____
_____
_____
_____
_____

170. what are you afraid of right now? How does it prevent you from moving forward?

_____

_____

_____

_____

_____

_____

_____

_____

_____

_____

_____

_____

_____

_____

_____

_____

_____

_____

_____

_____

_____

_____

_____

_____

_____

_____

_____

_____

171. Do you avoid making decisions out of fear of making bad choices? What are your options and possible outcomes?

_____

_____

_____

_____

_____

_____

_____

_____

_____

_____

_____

_____

_____

_____

_____

_____

_____

_____

_____

_____

_____

_____

_____

_____

_____

_____

_____

_____

_____

_____

172. Do you ever engage in self-sabotaging behaviors (actions that you know will have harmful repercussions, but you do them anyway)?

_____
_____
_____
_____
_____
_____
_____
_____
_____
_____
_____
_____
_____
_____
_____
_____
_____
_____
_____
_____
_____
_____
_____
_____
_____
_____
_____
_____
_____
_____
_____
_____

173. What are your biggest limiting thoughts about yourself? How does it keep you from moving forward?

_____

_____

_____

_____

_____

_____

_____

_____

_____

_____

_____

_____

_____

_____

_____

_____

_____

_____

_____

_____

_____

_____

_____

_____

_____

_____

_____

174. Are you afraid of making mistakes? Even if there is no "punish-ment"? Why or why not? How does that make you feel?

_____

_____

_____

_____

_____

_____

_____

_____

_____

_____

_____

_____

_____

_____

_____

_____

_____

_____

_____

_____

_____

_____

_____

_____

_____

_____

175. What would you do differently in your daily life if you knew that no one would judge you?

_____

_____

_____

_____

_____

_____

_____

_____

_____

_____

_____

_____

_____

_____

_____

_____

_____

_____

_____

_____

_____

_____

_____

_____

_____

_____

_____

_____

_____

176. What would you do if you had absolutely no fear?

_____

_____

_____

_____

_____

_____

_____

_____

_____

_____

_____

_____

_____

_____

_____

_____

_____

_____

_____

_____

_____

_____

_____

_____

_____

_____

_____

_____

_____

_____

_____

_____

DATE: _____   SUBJECT: FEAR

177. What would happen if you took an action to move one step closer to achieving the goal you are most anxious about?

_____

_____

_____

_____

_____

_____

_____

_____

_____

_____

_____

_____

_____

_____

_____

_____

_____

_____

_____

_____

_____

_____

_____

_____

_____

_____

_____

_____

_____

178. What will you do if you take action and it doesn't work as well as you thought?

_____

_____

_____

_____

_____

_____

_____

_____

_____

_____

_____

_____

_____

_____

_____

_____

_____

_____

_____

_____

_____

_____

_____

_____

_____

DATE: _____   SUBJECT: FEAR

179. What are you most afraid of right now? Write that fear down. Now imagine yourself overcoming that fear. How does it make you feel?

_____
_____
_____
_____
_____
_____
_____
_____
_____
_____
_____
_____
_____
_____
_____
_____
_____
_____
_____
_____
_____
_____
_____
_____
_____
_____
_____
_____
_____

180. If the thing you fear the most were to happen today, how would you feel? How would you react? What would be the solutions? Take a moment to objectively prepare for it.

_____

_____

_____

_____

_____

_____

_____

_____

_____

_____

_____

_____

_____

_____

_____

_____

_____

_____

_____

_____

_____

_____

_____

_____

_____

DATE: _____   SUBJECT: FEAR

181. What do you avoid because you are afraid?

_____
_____
_____
_____
_____
_____
_____
_____
_____
_____
_____
_____
_____
_____
_____
_____
_____
_____
_____
_____
_____
_____
_____
_____
_____
_____
_____
_____
_____
_____
_____
_____
_____
_____
_____

182. How much does your fear cost you in terms of health (physical and psychological) and well-being?

_____
_____
_____
_____
_____
_____
_____
_____
_____
_____
_____
_____
_____
_____
_____
_____
_____
_____
_____
_____
_____
_____
_____
_____
_____
_____
_____
_____
_____
_____
_____
_____
_____
_____

183. What advice would you give to a good friend who told you that they were too afraid to pursue their dreams because they were afraid of failing?

_____
_____
_____
_____
_____
_____
_____
_____
_____
_____
_____
_____
_____
_____
_____
_____
_____
_____
_____
_____
_____
_____
_____
_____
_____
_____
_____
_____
_____

184. What if you gave this same advice to yourself? How does it make you feel?

_____

_____

_____

_____

_____

_____

_____

_____

_____

_____

_____

_____

_____

_____

_____

_____

_____

_____

_____

_____

_____

_____

_____

_____

_____

_____

_____

_____

_____

185. Do your fears ever motivate you to act? Why or why not?

_____

_____

_____

_____

_____

_____

_____

_____

_____

_____

_____

_____

_____

_____

_____

_____

_____

_____

_____

_____

_____

_____

_____

_____

_____

_____

_____

_____

_____

_____

_____

_____

_____

186. Can you imagine your life if you did nothing and let fear hold you back all the time? What would it be like?

_____

_____

_____

_____

_____

_____

_____

_____

_____

_____

_____

_____

_____

_____

_____

_____

_____

_____

_____

_____

_____

_____

_____

_____

_____

_____

_____

_____

_____

DATE: _____   SUBJECT: FEAR

187. Do you believe the comments of others who tell you that "this is crazy" or "you shouldn't do this"? Why or why not?

_____
_____
_____
_____
_____
_____
_____
_____
_____
_____
_____
_____
_____
_____
_____
_____
_____
_____
_____
_____
_____
_____
_____
_____
_____
_____
_____

188. What harmful behaviors stop you from taking action?

_____

_____

_____

_____

_____

_____

_____

_____

_____

_____

_____

_____

_____

_____

_____

_____

_____

_____

_____

_____

_____

_____

_____

_____

_____

_____

_____

_____

_____

_____

DATE: _____   SUBJECT: FEAR

189. Are you currently in an unhappy, unhealthy or dysfunctional relationship that you are afraid to get out of? Why are you afraid?

_____
_____
_____
_____
_____
_____
_____
_____
_____
_____
_____
_____
_____
_____
_____
_____
_____
_____
_____
_____
_____
_____
_____
_____
_____
_____
_____
_____

190. Are you currently in a job that you are afraid to leave? Why or why not? If so, what deeper fear is it based on?

_____

_____

_____

_____

_____

_____

_____

_____

_____

_____

_____

_____

_____

_____

_____

_____

_____

_____

_____

_____

_____

_____

_____

_____

_____

_____

_____

_____

191. How do you feel about authority figures?

_____

_____

_____

_____

_____

_____

_____

_____

_____

_____

_____

_____

_____

_____

_____

_____

_____

_____

_____

_____

_____

_____

_____

_____

_____

_____

_____

_____

_____

_____

7

Obstacles

"Obstacles don't have to stop you.
If you run into a wall, don't turn around and give up.
Figure out how to climb it, go through it,
or work around it."
—— **Michael Jordan**

===

Ever since we started having control over our bodies (around 4 or 5months old), life has been filled with obstacles. Sometimes the obstacles are (metaphorically) a tree trunk in our path, or a 10 foot high brick wall. When we were babies, when we wanted to pick up an object, the obstacle was our not-so-perfect motor coordination. Then our lack of balance became an obstacle when we tried to walk upright. Educational toys are, in fact, designed to stimulate the brain to solve obstacles. Then comes school and educational learning. Friendships and misunderstandings. Things that don't go as planned. Last minute changes of plans.

In short, life is a series of obstacles. It never stops.

And you have two choices.

Either we stop moving forward because a wall is blocking our way (and we stay put or we turn back), or we find a way to go around it, over it or through it and we keep going.

It is clear that the first choice is the simple, easy choice. No effort, we drop and freeze or we turn back.
The second choice is the one that requires time, reflection, support, perseverance, courage. It's not necessarily more complicated, but because it's often more difficult, we tend to automatically see it as more complicated.

But if we always froze or turned back when we encountered a difficulty or an obstacle, we wouldn't have learned or accomplished much since our birth.
An obstacle is a blocked street when you run out of food and have to go to the supermarket.
Do you turn back and say to yourself "well too bad, looks like I won't eat.."?
Or do you find another way, even if it means arriving at the grocery store 10 minutes later than planned?
Or go home and order a pizza?

Obstacles are just that. It's something that happens in our path and if, when we were little, there was nothing that could stop us, it seems that the more we grow up, the more we prefer not to fight the obstacle (and feel sorry for ourselves).

But obstacles have always been an opportunity to learn and adapt.
Each obstacle allows us to develop something that will be useful for the rest of our life, that will make the rest easier, since we will be better equipped, cause it will become familiar ground.

But then, why do we let obstacles stop us in adulthood, when as a child or even as a toddler, it was a challenge?
What if we saw our obstacles as challenges instead, like before?
Literally soemthing to overcome?

Adaptation is an important part of tackling these challenges and a great quality to acquire in order to feel good about yourself and your life.

Having a momentary feeling of resistance to something unexpected, of course!

It is very valid to be upset when faced with an obstacle.

What will make the difference is our reaction once the shock has worn off.

Do we find a solution or do we turn back?

192. What are the obstacles you are currently facing?

_____

_____

_____

_____

_____

_____

_____

_____

_____

_____

_____

_____

_____

_____

_____

_____

_____

_____

_____

_____

_____

_____

_____

_____

_____

_____

_____

_____

_____

_____

_____

_____

DATE: _____   SUBJECT: OBSTACLES

193. Which of these obstacles have the greatest impact on you? Why do they impact you so much?

_____

_____

_____

_____

_____

_____

_____

_____

_____

_____

_____

_____

_____

_____

_____

_____

_____

_____

_____

_____

_____

_____

_____

_____

_____

_____

_____

194. Are you already doing anything to overcome these obstacles?

_____

_____

_____

_____

_____

_____

_____

_____

_____

_____

_____

_____

_____

_____

_____

_____

_____

_____

_____

_____

_____

_____

_____

_____

_____

_____

_____

_____

_____

_____

195. What more can you do to overcome these obstacles?

_____

_____

_____

_____

_____

_____

_____

_____

_____

_____

_____

_____

_____

_____

_____

_____

_____

_____

_____

_____

_____

_____

_____

_____

_____

_____

_____

_____

_____

_____

_____

_____

196. If the biggest obstacle in your life disappeared tomorrow morning, how would your life change?

_____

_____

_____

_____

_____

_____

_____

_____

_____

_____

_____

_____

_____

_____

_____

_____

_____

_____

_____

_____

_____

_____

_____

_____

_____

_____

_____

_____

_____

_____

DATE: _____   SUBJECT: OBSTACLES

197. What is the biggest obstacle you have had to overcome in your life?

_____
_____
_____
_____
_____
_____
_____
_____
_____
_____
_____
_____
_____
_____
_____
_____
_____
_____
_____
_____
_____
_____
_____
_____
_____
_____
_____
_____
_____
_____
_____

198. Is there anyone or anything that is stopping you from doing what you would like to do?

_____

_____

_____

_____

_____

_____

_____

_____

_____

_____

_____

_____

_____

_____

_____

_____

_____

_____

_____

_____

_____

_____

_____

_____

_____

_____

_____

_____

199. What prevents you from being 100% yourself?

_____

_____

_____

_____

_____

_____

_____

_____

_____

_____

_____

_____

_____

_____

_____

_____

_____

_____

_____

_____

_____

_____

_____

_____

_____

_____

_____

_____

_____

_____

_____

_____

_____

_____

SUBJECT: OBSTACLES

200. What obstacles do you encounter, only to realize that you put them there yourself?

_____
_____
_____
_____
_____
_____
_____
_____
_____
_____
_____
_____
_____
_____
_____
_____
_____
_____
_____
_____
_____
_____
_____
_____
_____
_____
_____
_____
_____
_____

201. Think of an obstacle you are currently facing. What do you find so difficult or overwhelming about this situation?

_____

_____

_____

_____

_____

_____

_____

_____

_____

_____

_____

_____

_____

_____

_____

_____

_____

_____

_____

_____

_____

_____

_____

_____

_____

_____

_____

202. In relation to the obstacles in your life, is there at least one thing you can do to take a step forward?

_____

_____

_____

_____

_____

_____

_____

_____

_____

_____

_____

_____

_____

_____

_____

_____

_____

_____

_____

_____

_____

_____

_____

_____

_____

_____

_____

_____

_____

203. How do you feel when you imagine yourself going ahead and doing this/these thing(s)?

_____

_____

_____

_____

_____

_____

_____

_____

_____

_____

_____

_____

_____

_____

_____

_____

_____

_____

_____

_____

_____

_____

_____

_____

_____

_____

_____

204. What obstacles have you helped others overcome?

_____

_____

_____

_____

_____

_____

_____

_____

_____

_____

_____

_____

_____

_____

_____

_____

_____

_____

_____

_____

_____

_____

_____

_____

_____

_____

_____

_____

_____

_____

_____

_____

_____

205. What obstacles do others have to overcome that you would naturally handle easily?

_____

_____

_____

_____

_____

_____

_____

_____

_____

_____

_____

_____

_____

_____

_____

_____

_____

_____

_____

_____

_____

_____

_____

_____

_____

_____

_____

_____

_____

206. What obstacles can you foresee in the future? How will you address them?

_____

_____

_____

_____

_____

_____

_____

_____

_____

_____

_____

_____

_____

_____

_____

_____

_____

_____

_____

_____

_____

_____

_____

_____

_____

_____

_____

_____

_____

207. How do you take care of yourself when you are going through
an ordeal?

_____

_____

_____

_____

_____

_____

_____

_____

_____

_____

_____

_____

_____

_____

_____

_____

_____

_____

_____

_____

_____

_____

_____

_____

_____

_____

_____

208. Talk about an obstacle that you had no control over at the beginning. How did you gain control? What will you do differently next time?

_____

_____

_____

_____

_____

_____

_____

_____

_____

_____

_____

_____

_____

_____

_____

_____

_____

_____

_____

_____

_____

_____

_____

_____

_____

_____

_____

_____

_____

209. Looking back, over what obstacles did you have more control than you thought?

_____

_____

_____

_____

_____

_____

_____

_____

_____

_____

_____

_____

_____

_____

_____

_____

_____

_____

_____

_____

_____

_____

_____

_____

_____

_____

_____

_____

_____

DATE: _____   SUBJECT: OBSTACLES

210. Who is (or are) the person(s) who has (have) helped you the most with your difficulties this year?

_____

_____

_____

_____

_____

_____

_____

_____

_____

_____

_____

_____

_____

_____

_____

_____

_____

_____

_____

_____

_____

_____

_____

_____

_____

_____

_____

_____

_____

_____

DATE: _____   SUBJECT: OBSTACLES

211. What valuable lessons have you learned from your obstacles?

_____

_____

_____

_____

_____

_____

_____

_____

_____

_____

_____

_____

_____

_____

_____

_____

_____

_____

_____

_____

_____

_____

_____

_____

_____

_____

_____

_____

_____

212. Do you agree to use the word "challenge" in place of "obstacle" or "problem" from now on? Why or why not?

_____

_____

_____

_____

_____

_____

_____

_____

_____

_____

_____

_____

_____

_____

_____

_____

_____

_____

_____

_____

_____

_____

_____

_____

_____

_____

_____

_____

_____

8

Changes

===

We are comfortable in our old slippers.

Sometimes the new shoes hurt our feet, but sometimes we accept the new, more padded pair with pleasure. Changes are often good, a breath of fresh air, but they can also be frightening and destabilizing. Even changes for the better can be destabilizing.

I hesitated for a long time to go see a psychologist. Not because of the stigma of "being crazy", not because "I should be able to handle it myself", not because I was burying my head in the sand thinking that I didn't need it, but because I was afraid. Afraid of the change in me. Afraid to get better. Afraid of not being me anymore, of not recognizing myself because I was going to be healed.

And later I heard other people share they had this same fear. Fear of getting lost if they went to therapy.

It's crazy, isn't it? To be afraid of being well inside because you're so used to being broken that you're afraid of not recognizing yourself anymore.

You know what I did?

Well, I didn't go see a shrink. I ran away from this threat of being healed.

It was many years later, after my studies in psychosocial therapy, that I realized that being well inside doesn't change you. You're still really you. With 100 pounds less on your shoulders and in your head, but still you. Life changes, or rather, your vision of life changes. Not you.

It's the colors outside that are brighter, it's the situations that are funnier and/or less annoying, it's the lilacs that smell better.
It's everything around us that is so much more pleasant.
　　Just imagine.
　　Something happens that would normally make us very angry and consumes lots of energy and one day, only makes us sigh, roll up our sleeves and adapt. We keep going.

We're just lighter. But we are still the same person at heart.

　　Like the caterpillar that becomes a butterfly, the buds that become flowers, the changes make us grow, make us blossom.

213. What is your relationship with change? Do you find it necessary or do you avoid change?

_____

_____

_____

_____

_____

_____

_____

_____

_____

_____

_____

_____

_____

_____

_____

_____

_____

_____

_____

_____

_____

_____

_____

_____

_____

_____

_____

_____

_____

_____

_____

214. Have you made any changes in your life recently? If so, what has been the impact? If not, are there any changes you would like to make?

215. What is the most difficult change you have had to go through?

_____

_____

_____

_____

_____

_____

_____

_____

_____

_____

_____

_____

_____

_____

_____

_____

_____

_____

_____

_____

_____

_____

_____

_____

_____

_____

_____

_____

_____

_____

_____

_____

_____

_____

216. What is the most beneficial change you have experienced?

_____

_____

_____

_____

_____

_____

_____

_____

_____

_____

_____

_____

_____

_____

_____

_____

_____

_____

_____

_____

_____

_____

_____

_____

_____

_____

_____

_____

_____

_____

_____

_____

_____

217. What is missing in your life right now?

_____

_____

_____

_____

_____

_____

_____

_____

_____

_____

_____

_____

_____

_____

_____

_____

_____

_____

_____

_____

_____

_____

_____

_____

_____

_____

_____

_____

_____

_____

_____

_____

_____

_____

_____

218. What would you like to change about your daily routine?

_____

_____

_____

_____

_____

_____

_____

_____

_____

_____

_____

_____

_____

_____

_____

_____

_____

_____

_____

_____

_____

_____

_____

_____

_____

_____

_____

_____

_____

_____

219. In relation to the previous question, what could you put into action this week to initiate these changes?

_____

_____

_____

_____

_____

_____

_____

_____

_____

_____

_____

_____

_____

_____

_____

_____

_____

_____

_____

_____

_____

_____

_____

_____

_____

_____

_____

_____

_____

_____

_____

220. What scares you about change?

_____

_____

_____

_____

_____

_____

_____

_____

_____

_____

_____

_____

_____

_____

_____

_____

_____

_____

_____

_____

_____

_____

_____

_____

_____

_____

_____

_____

_____

_____

_____

221. What change(s) in your daily life or in your behavior are you willing to make right now? What does this imply?

_____

_____

_____

_____

_____

_____

_____

_____

_____

_____

_____

_____

_____

_____

_____

_____

_____

_____

_____

_____

_____

_____

_____

_____

_____

_____

_____

_____

_____

222. What would be the risks or harmful impacts of refusing change?

_____

_____

_____

_____

_____

_____

_____

_____

_____

_____

_____

_____

_____

_____

_____

_____

_____

_____

_____

_____

_____

_____

_____

_____

_____

_____

_____

_____

_____

_____

_____

223. Sometimes the changes that occur are beyond our control. How easy is it for you to adapt? Has it always been at the same degree of ease?

_____

_____

_____

_____

_____

_____

_____

_____

_____

_____

_____

_____

_____

_____

_____

_____

_____

_____

_____

_____

_____

_____

_____

_____

_____

224. Is there any negativity that you would like to cut out of your life?
Will you dare? Why or why not?

_____

_____

_____

_____

_____

_____

_____

_____

_____

_____

_____

_____

_____

_____

_____

_____

_____

_____

_____

_____

_____

_____

_____

_____

_____

_____

_____

_____

_____

225. Resilience is accepting with serenity what you cannot control/ change. Share a time when you were resilient. List what was beneficial about being resilient.

_____

_____

_____

_____

_____

_____

_____

_____

_____

_____

_____

_____

_____

_____

_____

_____

_____

_____

_____

_____

_____

_____

_____

_____

_____

_____

_____

226. How do you deal with unexpected events that change your original plans on a daily basis? Why?

_____

_____

_____

_____

_____

_____

_____

_____

_____

_____

_____

_____

_____

_____

_____

_____

_____

_____

_____

_____

_____

_____

_____

_____

_____

_____

_____

DATE: _____   SUBJECT: CHANGES

227. What is the most unexpected change in your appearance that you
have ever made? How did you feel afterwards?

_____
_____
_____
_____
_____
_____
_____
_____
_____
_____
_____
_____
_____
_____
_____
_____
_____
_____
_____
_____
_____
_____
_____
_____
_____
_____
_____
_____
_____
_____

228. What is ONE thing you think will never change about you?

_____

_____

_____

_____

_____

_____

_____

_____

_____

_____

_____

_____

_____

_____

_____

_____

_____

_____

_____

_____

_____

_____

_____

_____

_____

_____

_____

_____

_____

_____

_____

229. What thing(s) have you tried to change, but it didn't work? Why do you think that is?

_____

_____

_____

_____

_____

_____

_____

_____

_____

_____

_____

_____

_____

_____

_____

_____

_____

_____

_____

_____

_____

_____

_____

_____

_____

_____

_____

_____

230. If you had $1 million tomorrow morning, what changes would you make in your life? Why?

_____

_____

_____

_____

_____

_____

_____

_____

_____

_____

_____

_____

_____

_____

_____

_____

_____

_____

_____

_____

_____

_____

_____

_____

_____

_____

_____

_____

_____

_____

_____

231. If you had $1 million tomorrow morning, what would you not change about your life? Why?

_____

_____

_____

_____

_____

_____

_____

_____

_____

_____

_____

_____

_____

_____

_____

_____

_____

_____

_____

_____

_____

_____

_____

_____

_____

_____

_____

_____

_____

_____

DATE: _____   SUBJECT: CHANGES

232. Have you ever decided to change the way you eat (food, schedule, etc.)? Why or why not?

_____
_____
_____
_____
_____
_____
_____
_____
_____
_____
_____
_____
_____
_____
_____
_____
_____
_____
_____
_____
_____
_____
_____
_____
_____
_____
_____

9

Regrets & Guilt

"You'll seldom experience regret for anything that you've done.
It is what you haven't done that will torment you.
he message, therefore, is clear. Do it!
Develop an appreciation for the present moment.
Seize every second of your life and savor it."
—— **Wayne Dyer**

==

The more I think about it, the more I delve into the concept of regret, remorse and guilt, the more I find them fascinating but also useless. Some feelings doesn't bring anything good to the table as they don't really inform us on a need. Yet these are feelings that many people have in many situations. Feelings that, I observe, are symptoms of something bigger, of a whole culture that still drags the lessons of Christianity and always those of capitalism.

Guilt is linked to judgment, including self-judgment. It is a hidden cultural aspect, linked to the fear of punishment from an authority, from society or from God. The imagined punishment can be physical or mental.

Society, religion and even family teach us values and goals for our lives. They dictate to us what a good human should think, do, be and want. We might see all this as an ideal to be achieved as a person, and it is the gap between this ideal and reality that gives rise to this feeling of guilt.

Guilt implies, by its definition, being guilty of a fault (failure to comply with a moral rule or a norm), or having the feeling of having made a fault. It is thus seen as a fault not to reach the ideal which one gives themselves or which is given to us, and we are guilty of this fault.

And this is precisely the problem. Our ideals seem to be the only possible option, without which it is a failure, a fault.

Am I a good son? A good friend? A good person? Do I live up to what I should be?

Because we judge people by the results (whether or not they achieve the goal) and not by the path (behaviors/choices/actions) towards the goal, our value as a human being is based on achieving the "ideal". Except that it is often impossible to predict with certainty the results of an action or a choice, results that often have impacts on other people and other domains and that can snowball.

And even our education system is based on this (think about how good or bad grades are received), just to reinforce the guilt feeling of "not being good enough".

But why would we want to reinforce this feeling?

Because humans are much more manipulable when they feel guilty.

Sometimes guilt arises for no other reason than that someone else is not happy with the impact of our action or words. We tell ourselves that we made a bad decision, a mistake, because the result is not what we wanted, or not 100% positive.

Guilt and regret take up a lot of space in people's hearts and minds, a weight that we carry around with us for most of our lives and that tints everything that comes after.

Is it possible to no longer live with guilt? Regret? Remorse? .... And still be a sensitive and compassionate person?

Of course it is!

We must first understand why we feel guilty, why we have regrets, and then work to implement the importance of actions, not results. Regardless of the results, if our actions were done to the best of our ability, to the best of our knowledge and with good intentions, we must be aware that there was no fault.

I hear you saying "the road to hell is paved with good intentions"... You see how the religion still have a big impact on our perceptions? Religion wants to see results, they don't care about the path taken (big red flag!) and has successfully taught us that whatever the intentions (and even knowledge!), if the result is not beneficial for someone, (usually for someone "more important than you") you did wrong.

But how can you act on something you don't know?
How can it be a mistake if you were not aware of a important information?

And even if we are the trigger of the snowball-events, we did the BEST we could at that moment and there is nothing else anyone can do. It's stressful to see the series of impacts triggered by something we've said or done, but once it is done, it's done and we only have control over ourselves and our actions, no control over the rest.

Let's take the next few days to question ourselves, to reflect on these feelings and their sources.

233. What does failure mean to you?

_____

_____

_____

_____

_____

_____

_____

_____

_____

_____

_____

_____

_____

_____

_____

_____

_____

_____

_____

_____

_____

_____

_____

_____

_____

_____

_____

_____

_____

_____

_____

_____

234. What does regret mean to you?

_____

_____

_____

_____

_____

_____

_____

_____

_____

_____

_____

_____

_____

_____

_____

_____

_____

_____

_____

_____

_____

_____

_____

_____

_____

_____

_____

_____

_____

_____

_____

_____

_____

235. Why is it difficult to face failure? What does it say about you? What judgment of yourself do you have at that moment?

_____

_____

_____

_____

_____

_____

_____

_____

_____

_____

_____

_____

_____

_____

_____

_____

_____

_____

_____

_____

_____

_____

_____

_____

_____

_____

_____

_____

_____

236. Tell about (a) time(s) when your parents, teachers, or other close people diminished or invalidated your choices/actions. How did this make you feel? What was the impact afterwards?

_____

_____

_____

_____

_____

_____

_____

_____

_____

_____

_____

_____

_____

_____

_____

_____

_____

_____

_____

_____

_____

_____

_____

_____

_____

_____

237. What have you given up/left go in your life that you still regret today? Why is this a regret?

_____

_____

_____

_____

_____

_____

_____

_____

_____

_____

_____

_____

_____

_____

_____

_____

_____

_____

_____

_____

_____

_____

_____

_____

_____

_____

_____

_____

_____

238. What do you wish you could quit without regret? What prevents you from doing so (besides regrets)?

_____

_____

_____

_____

_____

_____

_____

_____

_____

_____

_____

_____

_____

_____

_____

_____

_____

_____

_____

_____

_____

_____

_____

_____

_____

_____

_____

_____

_____

_____

DATE : _____   SUBJECT : REGRETS & GUILT

239. What do you think is your biggest source of guilt?

240. If today was your last day alive, would you have any regrets? If so, what would they be?

_____

_____

_____

_____

_____

_____

_____

_____

_____

_____

_____

_____

_____

_____

_____

_____

_____

_____

_____

_____

_____

_____

_____

_____

_____

_____

_____

_____

_____

241. In relation to the previous question, what could you do right now (even if it's the smallest step possible) to avoid carrying those regrets for the rest of your life?

_____

_____

_____

_____

_____

_____

_____

_____

_____

_____

_____

_____

_____

_____

_____

_____

_____

_____

_____

_____

_____

_____

_____

_____

_____

_____

_____

242. What makes you eventually forgive others? What "deserves" forgiveness on your part?

_____

_____

_____

_____

_____

_____

_____

_____

_____

_____

_____

_____

_____

_____

_____

_____

_____

_____

_____

_____

_____

_____

_____

_____

_____

_____

_____

_____

_____

243. Regarding the previous question, what if you had the same standard of forgiveness for yourself? What could you forgive yourself for?

_____
_____
_____
_____
_____
_____
_____
_____
_____
_____
_____
_____
_____
_____
_____
_____
_____
_____
_____
_____
_____
_____
_____
_____
_____
_____
_____

244. Tell about a time (or times) when your parents, teachers, or other close people rewarded or validated your choices or actions. How did this make you feel? What was the impact afterwards?

_____

_____

_____

_____

_____

_____

_____

_____

_____

_____

_____

_____

_____

_____

_____

_____

_____

_____

_____

_____

_____

_____

_____

_____

_____

245. Tell about a time when you did something and regretted not doing it before. Why didn't you do it before? What did you learn?

_____

_____

_____

_____

_____

_____

_____

_____

_____

_____

_____

_____

_____

_____

_____

_____

_____

_____

_____

_____

_____

_____

_____

_____

_____

_____

_____

_____

_____

DATE: _____   SUBJECT: REGRETS & GUILT

246. Where do you think your tendency to feel guilty comes from? What would be the solutions to get rid of it? If you don't feel guilty, what was your path to achieving this liberation?

_____
_____
_____
_____
_____
_____
_____
_____
_____
_____
_____
_____
_____
_____
_____
_____
_____
_____
_____
_____
_____
_____
_____
_____
_____
_____
_____

247. What is your relationship with perfectionism? What impact (beneficial or damaging) does your perfectionism (or lack thereof) have on your life?

_____
_____
_____
_____
_____
_____
_____
_____
_____
_____
_____
_____
_____
_____
_____
_____
_____
_____
_____
_____
_____
_____
_____
_____
_____
_____
_____

10

Humans Relationships

*"If civilization is to survive,
we must cultivate the science of human relationships -
the ability of all peoples, of all kinds,
to live together, in the same world at peace."*
—— **Franklin D. Roosevelt**

===

Before the internet, before technology, before wars and conquests of countries, before industrialization and working for a living, before politics and culture clashes, human relationships were already there, from the beginning, when humans were simply with humans, surviving, working together to build safe places to live. The human, alone with the human.

Even if it seems that we have evolved more than other animal species (I say "seems" because some animals leave us perplexed as to their intelligence and/or community spirit, like the crow, the dolphin, the octopus), the human remains a social species whose instinct, even if we tend not to listen to it sometimes, is the basis of our survival. So before anything else, humanity is the human with other humans. Human relations are of utmost importance in our development, in our evolution, both as a society and as an individual. Today, human relationships are part of the life landscape of everyone, but too often without paying much attention to them. Not that we don't pay attention to our family and friends, no, but we underestimate the psychological impact of relationships.

For example, in the name of the "family", we not only accept, but force ourselves to be surrounded by people whose behaviors have a damaging impact on us. We even excuse them, sometimes.

During a conference I attended with Dr. Serge Marquis (author, speaker and board-certified medicine physician), he told us that one of the main reasons we love our workplace is the people we work with.... and that one of the main reasons we hate our workplace is the people we worked with.
The people we see regularly have a huge impact on our mental health and we hang around collegues more than our friends sometimes.

While money doesn't make you zen in your body and mind (yeah, I know money can prevent A LOT of stress and it certainly help to seek inner peace but on itself, is not enough for true happiness), healthy and fulfilling human relationships are an important key to everyday happiness.

Debi Hope on Twitter said, in 2010, "before you are diagnosed with depression or low self-esteem, first make sure you are not, in fact, just surrounded by assholes," and she couldn't be more right.
Work, travel, passions, projects, spirituality and all other spheres have their role to play in a healthy and balanced life, but since human relationships is linked with many spheres (friendship, work, family, love, sexuality at least), it is essential to take the time to question ourselves on our relationships, on the degree of satisfaction of these relationships, on what we are looking for from them, etc.

248. Currently, which relationships (and with whom) are most valuable to you? Why are they important to you?

_____

_____

_____

_____

_____

_____

_____

_____

_____

_____

_____

_____

_____

_____

_____

_____

_____

_____

_____

_____

_____

_____

_____

_____

_____

_____

_____

_____

_____

249. In a similar fashion, which relationships (and with whom) are the most difficult right now? What makes them difficult?

_____

_____

_____

_____

_____

_____

_____

_____

_____

_____

_____

_____

_____

_____

_____

_____

_____

_____

_____

_____

_____

_____

_____

_____

_____

_____

_____

_____

250. Who do you want approval from? Who are you afraid of dis-appointing? Why?

_____

_____

_____

_____

_____

_____

_____

_____

_____

_____

_____

_____

_____

_____

_____

_____

_____

_____

_____

_____

_____

_____

_____

_____

_____

_____

_____

_____

_____

_____

DATE: _____ SUBJECT: HUMAN RELATIONS

251. What are the relationship(s) that you no longer have, but would like to have again? What did this/these relationship(s) bring you?

_____

_____

_____

_____

_____

_____

_____

_____

_____

_____

_____

_____

_____

_____

_____

_____

_____

_____

_____

_____

_____

_____

_____

_____

_____

_____

_____

_____

_____

252. What quality or personality trait do you most admire in others?

_____

_____

_____

_____

_____

_____

_____

_____

_____

_____

_____

_____

_____

_____

_____

_____

_____

_____

_____

_____

_____

_____

_____

_____

_____

_____

_____

_____

_____

_____

_____

253. What quality or personality trait irritates you most in others? How does this behavior/characteristic relate to you and your values?

_____
_____
_____
_____
_____
_____
_____
_____
_____
_____
_____
_____
_____
_____
_____
_____
_____
_____
_____
_____
_____
_____
_____
_____
_____
_____
_____
_____
_____
_____
_____
_____

254. With whom would you like to have a closer relationship? Why?

_____

_____

_____

_____

_____

_____

_____

_____

_____

_____

_____

_____

_____

_____

_____

_____

_____

_____

_____

_____

_____

_____

_____

_____

_____

_____

_____

_____

_____

DATE: _____   SUBJECT: HUMAN RELATIONS

255. How do you behave in conflicts that concern you?

_____
_____
_____
_____
_____
_____
_____
_____
_____
_____
_____
_____
_____
_____
_____
_____
_____
_____
_____
_____
_____
_____
_____
_____
_____
_____
_____
_____
_____
_____
_____
_____
_____

DATE: _____   SUBJECT: HUMAN RELATIONS

256. List the boundaries you would like to set with the people around you.

_____
_____
_____
_____
_____
_____
_____
_____
_____
_____
_____
_____
_____
_____
_____
_____
_____
_____
_____
_____
_____
_____
_____
_____
_____
_____
_____
_____
_____
_____

257. Do you have a grudge against someone right now? If yes, explain
why. If not, how do you manage to avoid holding grudges?

_____

_____

_____

_____

_____

_____

_____

_____

_____

_____

_____

_____

_____

_____

_____

_____

_____

_____

_____

_____

_____

_____

_____

_____

_____

_____

_____

_____

258. Think of a time when you have been hurt, angry, or felt dis-respected by someone. List any possible reasons that are not directly against you that could explain this behavior.

_____

_____

_____

_____

_____

_____

_____

_____

_____

_____

_____

_____

_____

_____

_____

_____

_____

_____

_____

_____

_____

_____

_____

_____

_____

_____

_____

259. Think of a person around you who drains you of energy, makes you cry often or makes you angry. Why does this person still have access to your life?

_____

_____

_____

_____

_____

_____

_____

_____

_____

_____

_____

_____

_____

_____

_____

_____

_____

_____

_____

_____

_____

_____

_____

_____

_____

_____

DATE: _____   SUBJECT: HUMAN RELATIONS

260. Describe your dream social life. What could you do to get there/
what did you do to get there?

_____

_____

_____

_____

_____

_____

_____

_____

_____

_____

_____

_____

_____

_____

_____

_____

_____

_____

_____

_____

_____

_____

_____

_____

_____

_____

_____

_____

_____

_____

_____

261. Who makes you feel your best? Recharged with energy?

_____

_____

_____

_____

_____

_____

_____

_____

_____

_____

_____

_____

_____

_____

_____

_____

_____

_____

_____

_____

_____

_____

_____

_____

_____

_____

_____

_____

_____

_____

_____

_____

_____

_____

262. Recall a success you experienced and write a thank you letter to the person who had the greatest beneficial impact for you in the situation. Bonus point if you send it to them ;)

_____
_____
_____
_____
_____
_____
_____
_____
_____
_____
_____
_____
_____
_____
_____
_____
_____
_____
_____
_____
_____
_____
_____
_____
_____
_____
_____
_____

263. Who has made you smile in the last 24 hours? Why? What happened?

_____

_____

_____

_____

_____

_____

_____

_____

_____

_____

_____

_____

_____

_____

_____

_____

_____

_____

_____

_____

_____

_____

_____

_____

_____

_____

_____

_____

_____

_____

DATE: _____   SUBJECT: HUMAN RELATIONS

264. Think of something you would like to accomplish in the medium term. Who can help you achieve this goal?

_____

_____

_____

_____

_____

_____

_____

_____

_____

_____

_____

_____

_____

_____

_____

_____

_____

_____

_____

_____

_____

_____

_____

_____

_____

265. Who has had the biggest impact on your life? Why and what is that impact?

_____

_____

_____

_____

_____

_____

_____

_____

_____

_____

_____

_____

_____

_____

_____

_____

_____

_____

_____

_____

_____

_____

_____

_____

_____

_____

_____

_____

266. Does it really matter what other people think of you? Why or why not?

_____

_____

_____

_____

_____

_____

_____

_____

_____

_____

_____

_____

_____

_____

_____

_____

_____

_____

_____

_____

_____

_____

_____

_____

_____

_____

_____

_____

267. In what ways is the public "you" different from the private "you"?

268. When, where and with whom do you feel 100% yourself?

_____

_____

_____

_____

_____

_____

_____

_____

_____

_____

_____

_____

_____

_____

_____

_____

_____

_____

_____

_____

_____

_____

_____

_____

_____

_____

_____

_____

_____

_____

269. Who are the people who support you most in life?

_____

_____

_____

_____

_____

_____

_____

_____

_____

_____

_____

_____

_____

_____

_____

_____

_____

_____

_____

_____

_____

_____

_____

_____

_____

_____

_____

_____

_____

_____

_____

270. What does being a good friend mean to you? What are your expectations of a friend?

_____

_____

_____

_____

_____

_____

_____

_____

_____

_____

_____

_____

_____

_____

_____

_____

_____

_____

_____

_____

_____

_____

_____

_____

_____

_____

_____

_____

DATE: _____ SUBJECT: HUMAN RELATIONS

271. What expectations do you have of yourself in relation to the people around you (family/friends)?

_____

_____

_____

_____

_____

_____

_____

_____

_____

_____

_____

_____

_____

_____

_____

_____

_____

_____

_____

_____

_____

_____

_____

_____

_____

_____

_____

272. Tell us about the best relationship (family, friendship or love) you have ever had. How was it different from all the others?

_____

_____

_____

_____

_____

_____

_____

_____

_____

_____

_____

_____

_____

_____

_____

_____

_____

_____

_____

_____

_____

_____

_____

_____

_____

_____

_____

_____

_____

_____

_____

_____

273. Think about your last romantic relationship. Why did you choose this particular person? If you have never been in a relationship, what are the things you want to find in the other person?

_____

_____

_____

_____

_____

_____

_____

_____

_____

_____

_____

_____

_____

_____

_____

_____

_____

_____

_____

_____

_____

_____

_____

_____

_____

_____

_____

_____

_____

_____

DATE: _____   SUBJECT: HUMAN RELATIONS

274. In what situations have you not dared to ask for help or confide in those closest to you? Why?

_____

_____

_____

_____

_____

_____

_____

_____

_____

_____

_____

_____

_____

_____

_____

_____

_____

_____

_____

_____

_____

_____

_____

_____

_____

_____

_____

275. What relationships do you neglect? Why? How does this make you feel?

_____

_____

_____

_____

_____

_____

_____

_____

_____

_____

_____

_____

_____

_____

_____

_____

_____

_____

_____

_____

_____

_____

_____

_____

_____

_____

_____

276. How do you let the needs and desires of others dictate your choices and actions? Why do you do this?

_____

_____

_____

_____

_____

_____

_____

_____

_____

_____

_____

_____

_____

_____

_____

_____

_____

_____

_____

_____

_____

_____

_____

_____

_____

_____

_____

_____

_____

_____

_____

277. What, if any, confrontations do you avoid? And why?

_____

_____

_____

_____

_____

_____

_____

_____

_____

_____

_____

_____

_____

_____

_____

_____

_____

_____

_____

_____

_____

_____

_____

_____

_____

_____

_____

_____

_____

_____

278. Which of your relationships drain your energy, stress you out, or depress you the most? Why do you keep them in your life?

_____

_____

_____

_____

_____

_____

_____

_____

_____

_____

_____

_____

_____

_____

_____

_____

_____

_____

_____

_____

_____

_____

_____

_____

_____

_____

_____

_____

_____

279. In relation to the previous question, what would happen if you decided to end these relationships?

_____

_____

_____

_____

_____

_____

_____

_____

_____

_____

_____

_____

_____

_____

_____

_____

_____

_____

_____

_____

_____

_____

_____

_____

_____

_____

_____

_____

_____

280. Why is it hard to say "no"? What would happen if you were more assertive?

_____

_____

_____

_____

_____

_____

_____

_____

_____

_____

_____

_____

_____

_____

_____

_____

_____

_____

_____

_____

_____

_____

_____

_____

_____

_____

_____

_____

_____

11

Empowerment

==

Empowerment is the foundation of social work. It means giving people the power over their lives back . Often, we don't even realize that we are no longer in control (or not in control enough), but there are signs that can alert us : feeling irritated, dissatisfied, complaining.

As a psychosocial practitioner, my role is to accompany people as they become the main actors of their lives and make the necessary changes to find serenity and good psychological health.
Empowerment is knowing in our gut that we are the captain of our ship. It's not just a "well yeah this is my life I do what I want", but more of a "Wow... I can really build my life in my image!"

A life where you don't feel stuck in a situation or relationship that doesn't fit you. A life where, if something no longer pleases you or allows you to thrive, you change it, detach from it and move on.
There are not only pleasant things that happen in life, either. An

empowered life is not always a pleasant life, without obstacles or difficulties. When we feel that we have control over ourselves and our life, that we really feel it, even if we have stress or if we find ourselves in front of a wall, there are two empowered options. Either we find a way to keep moving forward, or we turn back because we don't feel like it and move on. To be empowered is to know that what happens makes us grow. It's knowing that adapting and being resilient to what we can't change is the key to a rewarding and zen life.

It's feeling like you are truly in control of your life, even if you can't control the waves.

But before arriving at such a reflection, there are many questions to ask, there is a journey to make, a knowledge of ourselves but also a (re?)taking of the responsibility of our life.

And it is never too late to start. It's normal, even, to make this realization in adulthood because it's not something we're taught, nor encouraged to do.

We won't enter into therapy with this book, but if it can start a reflection in that sense, it's already a good thing!

281. Why do you get up every morning? What are the elements you 100% chose in these reasons?

_____
_____
_____
_____
_____
_____
_____
_____
_____
_____
_____
_____
_____
_____
_____
_____
_____
_____
_____
_____
_____
_____
_____
_____
_____
_____
_____

DATE: _____   SUBJECT: EMPOWERMENT

282. What makes you excited about your life right now?

_____

_____

_____

_____

_____

_____

_____

_____

_____

_____

_____

_____

_____

_____

_____

_____

_____

_____

_____

_____

_____

_____

_____

_____

_____

_____

_____

_____

_____

_____

_____

_____

283. In what areas do you feel you do not have control in your life? Why?

_____

_____

_____

_____

_____

_____

_____

_____

_____

_____

_____

_____

_____

_____

_____

_____

_____

_____

_____

_____

_____

_____

_____

_____

_____

_____

284. In relation to the previous question, where might you have a tiny bit of control (directly or indirectly) despite what appears at first glance?

285. Who do you fear to disappoint in life? Who has the power to influence your decisions in a direction you don't fully agree with?

_____

_____

_____

_____

_____

_____

_____

_____

_____

_____

_____

_____

_____

_____

_____

_____

_____

_____

_____

_____

_____

_____

_____

_____

_____

_____

_____

DATE: _____   SUBJECT: EMPOWERMENT

286. Look around you. Everything around you, the people, the objects, the place, are the result of a decision you have made to buy it, to have it, to create it, to keep it, or to tolerate it. What do you tolerate?

_____
_____
_____
_____
_____
_____
_____
_____
_____
_____
_____
_____
_____
_____
_____
_____
_____
_____
_____
_____
_____
_____
_____
_____
_____
_____
_____

287. Do you feel that your life is 100% your choices and decisions? If not, what percentage do you feel your life is?

_____
_____
_____
_____
_____
_____
_____
_____
_____
_____
_____
_____
_____
_____
_____
_____
_____
_____
_____
_____
_____
_____
_____
_____
_____
_____
_____
_____
_____

288. Are you the center of your own life? Why or why not?

_____
_____
_____
_____
_____
_____
_____
_____
_____
_____
_____
_____
_____
_____
_____
_____
_____
_____
_____
_____
_____
_____
_____
_____
_____
_____
_____
_____
_____
_____
_____
_____

289. Under what circumstances do you feel most empowered, in control?

_____

_____

_____

_____

_____

_____

_____

_____

_____

_____

_____

_____

_____

_____

_____

_____

_____

_____

_____

_____

_____

_____

_____

_____

_____

_____

_____

_____

_____

_____

DATE: _____   SUBJECT: EMPOWERMENT

290. Are your actions and decisions guided by fear, faith, or other factors?

_____
_____
_____
_____
_____
_____
_____
_____
_____
_____
_____
_____
_____
_____
_____
_____
_____
_____
_____
_____
_____
_____
_____
_____
_____
_____
_____
_____

291. Tell about a time when you pushed the limits (without stepping out of them) of your comfort zone. What did you learn?

_____
_____
_____
_____
_____
_____
_____
_____
_____
_____
_____
_____
_____
_____
_____
_____
_____
_____
_____
_____
_____
_____
_____
_____
_____
_____
_____
_____
_____
_____

292. How would you like to contribute, to leave your mark, in your family, social circle, community, city, world?

_____
_____
_____
_____
_____
_____
_____
_____
_____
_____
_____
_____
_____
_____
_____
_____
_____
_____
_____
_____
_____
_____
_____
_____
_____
_____

293. How is your life more positive today than it was 1 year ago?

_____

_____

_____

_____

_____

_____

_____

_____

_____

_____

_____

_____

_____

_____

_____

_____

_____

_____

_____

_____

_____

_____

_____

_____

_____

_____

_____

_____

_____

_____

_____

_____

_____

294. Do you feel that you are using your time as you would like to? Why or why not? If not, what could you do to improve this?

_____

_____

_____

_____

_____

_____

_____

_____

_____

_____

_____

_____

_____

_____

_____

_____

_____

_____

_____

_____

_____

_____

_____

_____

_____

_____

_____

_____

_____

DATE: _____ SUBJECT: EMPOWERMENT

295. How do you take care of yourself, physically, psychologically and emotionally?

_____
_____
_____
_____
_____
_____
_____
_____
_____
_____
_____
_____
_____
_____
_____
_____
_____
_____
_____
_____
_____
_____
_____
_____
_____
_____
_____
_____
_____
_____

296. There is a past version of yourself that wished with all its heart to have something that you have today. What is it?

_____
_____
_____
_____
_____
_____
_____
_____
_____
_____
_____
_____
_____
_____
_____
_____
_____
_____
_____
_____
_____
_____
_____
_____
_____
_____
_____
_____

297. What do you want to spend more time on each day? Why? What is stopping you from doing so?

_____

_____

_____

_____

_____

_____

_____

_____

_____

_____

_____

_____

_____

_____

_____

_____

_____

_____

_____

_____

_____

_____

_____

_____

_____

_____

_____

_____

_____

298. On the other hand, what would you like to spend less time doing each day? Why don't you do it?

_____

_____

_____

_____

_____

_____

_____

_____

_____

_____

_____

_____

_____

_____

_____

_____

_____

_____

_____

_____

_____

_____

_____

_____

_____

_____

_____

_____

_____

_____

299. How would you like to feel on a daily basis? Why?

_____

_____

_____

_____

_____

_____

_____

_____

_____

_____

_____

_____

_____

_____

_____

_____

_____

_____

_____

_____

_____

_____

_____

_____

_____

_____

_____

_____

300. What does it mean to you to be "successful in life"? Where does this definitions come from?

_____

_____

_____

_____

_____

_____

_____

_____

_____

_____

_____

_____

_____

_____

_____

_____

_____

_____

_____

_____

_____

_____

_____

_____

_____

_____

_____

_____

_____

_____

_____

301. How and in what ways are you different today than you were 5 years ago?

_____

_____

_____

_____

_____

_____

_____

_____

_____

_____

_____

_____

_____

_____

_____

_____

_____

_____

_____

_____

_____

_____

_____

_____

_____

_____

_____

_____

302. Do you like the person you are? What could you do to get a little closer to your ideal "you"?

_____

_____

_____

_____

_____

_____

_____

_____

_____

_____

_____

_____

_____

_____

_____

_____

_____

_____

_____

_____

_____

_____

_____

_____

_____

_____

_____

_____

_____

_____

303. Why did you choose the occupation (job, school, stay-at-home parent, etc.) you have? How does it make use of your strengths and talents?

_____

_____

_____

_____

_____

_____

_____

_____

_____

_____

_____

_____

_____

_____

_____

_____

_____

_____

_____

_____

_____

_____

_____

_____

_____

304. Talk about a time where you exceeded your own expectations.

_____

_____

_____

_____

_____

_____

_____

_____

_____

_____

_____

_____

_____

_____

_____

_____

_____

_____

_____

_____

_____

_____

_____

_____

_____

_____

_____

_____

_____

_____

_____

_____

DATE: _____   SUBJECT: EMPOWERMENT

305. When have you excelled where others around you have struggled?

_____

_____

_____

_____

_____

_____

_____

_____

_____

_____

_____

_____

_____

_____

_____

_____

_____

_____

_____

_____

_____

_____

_____

_____

_____

_____

_____

_____

306. Who are you most jealous of/envious of and why?

_____

_____

_____

_____

_____

_____

_____

_____

_____

_____

_____

_____

_____

_____

_____

_____

_____

_____

_____

_____

_____

_____

_____

_____

_____

_____

_____

_____

_____

_____

_____

307. What is your definition of happiness? What concrete actions are you taking to build it?

_____

_____

_____

_____

_____

_____

_____

_____

_____

_____

_____

_____

_____

_____

_____

_____

_____

_____

_____

_____

_____

_____

_____

_____

_____

_____

_____

_____

_____

_____

308. In what ways do you block your own happiness (i.e. self-sabotage)?

_____

_____

_____

_____

_____

_____

_____

_____

_____

_____

_____

_____

_____

_____

_____

_____

_____

_____

_____

_____

_____

_____

_____

_____

_____

_____

_____

_____

_____

_____

_____

_____

309. How often do you treat yourself with love and respect?

_____

_____

_____

_____

_____

_____

_____

_____

_____

_____

_____

_____

_____

_____

_____

_____

_____

_____

_____

_____

_____

_____

_____

_____

_____

_____

_____

_____

_____

_____

_____

_____

_____

310. How do you feel when you look in the mirror?

_____

_____

_____

_____

_____

_____

_____

_____

_____

_____

_____

_____

_____

_____

_____

_____

_____

_____

_____

_____

_____

_____

_____

_____

_____

_____

_____

_____

_____

_____

_____

_____

DATE: _____   SUBJECT: EMPOWERMENT

311. How do you contribute to your family, business or community?

_____

_____

_____

_____

_____

_____

_____

_____

_____

_____

_____

_____

_____

_____

_____

_____

_____

_____

_____

_____

_____

_____

_____

_____

_____

_____

_____

_____

_____

_____

_____

312. What are your strategies for getting back up after a disappoint-
ment/obstacle?

_____

_____

_____

_____

_____

_____

_____

_____

_____

_____

_____

_____

_____

_____

_____

_____

_____

_____

_____

_____

_____

_____

_____

_____

_____

_____

_____

_____

_____

313. What compliment do you like to receive the most and why?

_____

_____

_____

_____

_____

_____

_____

_____

_____

_____

_____

_____

_____

_____

_____

_____

_____

_____

_____

_____

_____

_____

_____

_____

_____

_____

_____

_____

_____

_____

_____

_____

_____

DATE: _____   SUBJECT: EMPOWERMENT

314. What is more important to you : <u>how your life looks to others</u> **or** <u>how your life makes you feel</u>?

_____

_____

_____

_____

_____

_____

_____

_____

_____

_____

_____

_____

_____

_____

_____

_____

_____

_____

_____

_____

_____

_____

_____

_____

_____

_____

_____

_____

_____

_____

_____

315. When was the last time you tried something new? How did it go? What did you learn?

_____

_____

_____

_____

_____

_____

_____

_____

_____

_____

_____

_____

_____

_____

_____

_____

_____

_____

_____

_____

_____

_____

_____

_____

_____

_____

_____

_____

316. Are you always trying to know more about yourself, others, society, or are you content with what you already know? Why?

_____

_____

_____

_____

_____

_____

_____

_____

_____

_____

_____

_____

_____

_____

_____

_____

_____

_____

_____

_____

_____

_____

_____

_____

_____

_____

_____

_____

_____

317. Name one belief you have that many people disagree with. Where does it come from? Why do you hold on to it?

_____
_____
_____
_____
_____
_____
_____
_____
_____
_____
_____
_____
_____
_____
_____
_____
_____
_____
_____
_____
_____
_____
_____
_____
_____
_____
_____
_____
_____

DATE: _____   SUBJECT: EMPOWERMENT

318. What can you do today that you were not able to do a year ago?

_____
_____
_____
_____
_____
_____
_____
_____
_____
_____
_____
_____
_____
_____
_____
_____
_____
_____
_____
_____
_____
_____
_____
_____
_____
_____
_____
_____
_____
_____

319. What is the difference between living and existing?

_____

_____

_____

_____

_____

_____

_____

_____

_____

_____

_____

_____

_____

_____

_____

_____

_____

_____

_____

_____

_____

_____

_____

_____

_____

_____

_____

_____

_____

_____

_____

_____

_____

_____

_____

320. If you had a friend who talked to you the way you talk to yourself, how long would you allow that person to be your friend?

_____

_____

_____

_____

_____

_____

_____

_____

_____

_____

_____

_____

_____

_____

_____

_____

_____

_____

_____

_____

_____

_____

_____

_____

_____

_____

_____

321. When you are 80 years old, what will have been the most important thing in your life?

_____

_____

_____

_____

_____

_____

_____

_____

_____

_____

_____

_____

_____

_____

_____

_____

_____

_____

_____

_____

_____

_____

_____

_____

_____

_____

_____

_____

_____

_____

_____

_____

_____

322. If you had the opportunity to deliver a message to a large group of people, what would your message be?

_____

_____

_____

_____

_____

_____

_____

_____

_____

_____

_____

_____

_____

_____

_____

_____

_____

_____

_____

_____

_____

_____

_____

_____

_____

_____

_____

_____

_____

DATE: _____   SUBJECT: EMPOWERMENT

323. What has life taught you recently?

_____

_____

_____

_____

_____

_____

_____

_____

_____

_____

_____

_____

_____

_____

_____

_____

_____

_____

_____

_____

_____

_____

_____

_____

_____

_____

_____

_____

_____

_____

_____

324. If we learn from our mistakes, why are we still so afraid to make a mistake?

_____

_____

_____

_____

_____

_____

_____

_____

_____

_____

_____

_____

_____

_____

_____

_____

_____

_____

_____

_____

_____

_____

_____

_____

_____

_____

_____

_____

_____

_____

12

The Future

===

The past is over and the future is yet to be built. Isn't that exciting? All these possibilities in front of us!
The future is like painting a canvas. We don't all have the same canvas, we don't all have the same brushes or colors, and we don't all have the same painting skills. Some have only the 3 primary colors, and others have the whole color palette. Some have watercolor or acrylic paint, others have oil paint. But we all have, at the very least, a surface to paint on, some brushes and some colors.

Every decision we make every day is a brush stroke on the canvas. It's easier to go over acrylics. It dries in 2 minutes and every bad brushstroke can be quickly corrected. With oil paint, you either use a pallet knife to remove the paint, or you wait two weeks for it to dry before painting over it. The important thing to remember, though, is that you can always paint over it. Sometimes it just takes longer. It's also possible to see the relief of the old layers of paint through the new ones, but from a distance, it won't look like much.

Just because we've made a choice or taken a direction doesn't mean we have to continue in the same direction if we're no longer satisfied. Our decisions and actions may leave small marks in our lives, the impacts of which are felt years later, like the relief of an old brush stroke, but in the grand scheme of life, of our canvas, these impacts are minor.

Moral of the analogy : We don't choose which tools we start with. But we are completely the Master of what we do with our tools. We can insist on staying with our 3 colors and painting on rocks, or we can approach people and share our colors with them, paint on their canvases with them, learn from their techniques, borrow their brushes, etc. We can look at other people's work and envy them, or study what they do for inspiration. We can save up and go shopping spree in an art store. No matter what's on our canvas, wooden slab or rock, we can always paint over it to make a new work of art.

This is the future. That's the artwork we're going to paint. And what's already on our canvas doesn't dictate what the final piece will be.

"Yeah, but I don't have any blue. And I don't know anyone who has blue. And I don't have the money to buy it. How do you expect me to make a beautiful sky?"

Have you ever seen a summer sunset? With shades of purple, pink and orange? Beautiful! And there is no blue. Well... there is in the purple but... if you already have purple.. Anyway, you get the idea.

Also, Bob Ross once painted a beautiful landscape in black and white!

We don't have the power to transform our wood board into a pre-primed 4 by 7 canvas, nor to make the color we want appear, but we can work to get that canvas, that color or adapt to make fabulous art despite the restrictions.

Have a quick glance at rock paintings and you'll see that we can make masterpieces on many things!

Some people are going to be happy all their lives drawing stick figures, because they have fun and that's what's important, and others aim for the Michelangelo painting. We're not all going to end up with the same canvas and the important thing is to see how much we've done to get where we are.

We are each the masters of our own future, no matter what we've been given in our lives so far, no matter what decisions we've made. From now on, right here, right now, we have the power to change everything to something completely different, something much more in our image.

DATE: _____   SUBJECT: THE FUTURE

325. What can you do today that will be a step closer to one of your dreams?

_____

_____

_____

_____

_____

_____

_____

_____

_____

_____

_____

_____

_____

_____

_____

_____

_____

_____

_____

_____

_____

_____

_____

_____

_____

_____

_____

_____

_____

DATE: _____   SUBJECT: THE FUTURE

326. What would you like to leave behind after you die?

_____

_____

_____

_____

_____

_____

_____

_____

_____

_____

_____

_____

_____

_____

_____

_____

_____

_____

_____

_____

_____

_____

_____

_____

_____

_____

_____

_____

_____

_____

_____

_____

_____

327. Instead of listing the things you don't want to happen in the future, list the things you would like to happen.

_____
_____
_____
_____
_____
_____
_____
_____
_____
_____
_____
_____
_____
_____
_____
_____
_____
_____
_____
_____
_____
_____
_____
_____
_____
_____
_____
_____
_____
_____

328. What skills do you want to acquire in the next five years?

DATE: _____   SUBJECT: THE FUTURE

329. Where will your life be in one, five or ten years if you continue to do what you are doing today?

_____

_____

_____

_____

_____

_____

_____

_____

_____

_____

_____

_____

_____

_____

_____

_____

_____

_____

_____

_____

_____

_____

_____

_____

_____

_____

_____

_____

_____

_____

330. Complete the sentence: I will be really happy in life when ...

_____

_____

_____

_____

_____

_____

_____

_____

_____

_____

_____

_____

_____

_____

_____

_____

_____

_____

_____

_____

_____

_____

_____

_____

_____

_____

331. What does a normal day look like for your ideal future you?

_____

_____

_____

_____

_____

_____

_____

_____

_____

_____

_____

_____

_____

_____

_____

_____

_____

_____

_____

_____

_____

_____

_____

_____

_____

_____

_____

_____

_____

_____

_____

_____

332. What do you want people to say about your ideal future self?

_____

_____

_____

_____

_____

_____

_____

_____

_____

_____

_____

_____

_____

_____

_____

_____

_____

_____

_____

_____

_____

_____

_____

_____

_____

_____

_____

_____

_____

_____

_____

_____

_____

_____

333. What habits would your future have, in your vision, that you do not have today? What should you do to move toward that goal?

_____

_____

_____

_____

_____

_____

_____

_____

_____

_____

_____

_____

_____

_____

_____

_____

_____

_____

_____

_____

_____

_____

_____

_____

_____

_____

_____

_____

_____

334. What worries you about the future? Why? What can you do to prevent these worries from happening?

_____

_____

_____

_____

_____

_____

_____

_____

_____

_____

_____

_____

_____

_____

_____

_____

_____

_____

_____

_____

_____

_____

_____

_____

_____

_____

_____

_____

_____

_____

13

Here and Now

"Be patient with yourself.
You are growing stronger every day.
The weight of the world will become lighter...
and you will begin to shine brighter.
Don't give up."
—— **Robert Tew**

==

Wow!
It's been almost a year since you started this introspection exercise, where you surely realized a lot of things, by going deeper into your feelings, your values, your needs. We change so much in life, I thought it would be really interesting to do a "here and now" again almost a year later to see the evolution.

So I suggest you answer the following questions (which are, for the most part, the same as part 2), always with as much precision and intro-spection as possible.

To really get the full picture of the changes that have begun in you, don't read the answers you wrote at the beginning of the year before answering these. Better yet, wait until you've answered the rest of the questions before you compare them to the beginning of the year. We evolve a lot more than we think, we just don't keep track of it.

If you enjoyed the experience, I invite you to repeat the introspection exercise regularly!
After several years, you will have a clear vision of all the inner journey you have made and the positive impacts it has had in your life :)

335. How do you feel when you wake up in the morning?

_____

_____

_____

_____

_____

_____

_____

_____

_____

_____

_____

_____

_____

_____

_____

_____

_____

_____

_____

_____

_____

_____

_____

_____

_____

_____

_____

_____

_____

_____

_____

_____

336. What takes up the majority of your time during the day other than work/school?

_____
_____
_____
_____
_____
_____
_____
_____
_____
_____
_____
_____
_____
_____
_____
_____
_____
_____
_____
_____
_____
_____
_____
_____
_____
_____
_____
_____
_____

337. What is the most difficult thing to accept about yourself?

_____

_____

_____

_____

_____

_____

_____

_____

_____

_____

_____

_____

_____

_____

_____

_____

_____

_____

_____

_____

_____

_____

_____

_____

_____

_____

_____

_____

_____

_____

_____

_____

_____

DATE : _____   SUBJECT : HERE & NOW

338. What matters most to you?

_____
_____
_____
_____
_____
_____
_____
_____
_____
_____
_____
_____
_____
_____
_____
_____
_____
_____
_____
_____
_____
_____
_____
_____
_____
_____
_____
_____
_____
_____
_____
_____
_____
_____
_____

339. What makes you feel energized, renewed and recharged?

_____
_____
_____
_____
_____
_____
_____
_____
_____
_____
_____
_____
_____
_____
_____
_____
_____
_____
_____
_____
_____
_____
_____
_____
_____
_____
_____
_____
_____
_____
_____
_____
_____

DATE : _____   SUBJECT : HERE & NOW

340. How do you spend your free time?

_____
_____
_____
_____
_____
_____
_____
_____
_____
_____
_____
_____
_____
_____
_____
_____
_____
_____
_____
_____
_____
_____
_____
_____
_____
_____
_____
_____
_____

341. How would you like to spend your free time?

_____

_____

_____

_____

_____

_____

_____

_____

_____

_____

_____

_____

_____

_____

_____

_____

_____

_____

_____

_____

_____

_____

_____

_____

_____

_____

_____

_____

_____

_____

_____

342. What are you passionate about (a topic or area you can't get enough of learning about and/or talking about)

_____
_____
_____
_____
_____
_____
_____
_____
_____
_____
_____
_____
_____
_____
_____
_____
_____
_____
_____
_____
_____
_____
_____
_____
_____
_____
_____
_____
_____

343. How much control do you feel you have in your daily life?

_____

_____

_____

_____

_____

_____

_____

_____

_____

_____

_____

_____

_____

_____

_____

_____

_____

_____

_____

_____

_____

_____

_____

_____

_____

_____

_____

_____

_____

_____

_____

_____

_____

344. What are you proud to have changed or developed in the past year?

_____

_____

_____

_____

_____

_____

_____

_____

_____

_____

_____

_____

_____

_____

_____

_____

_____

_____

_____

_____

_____

_____

_____

_____

_____

_____

_____

_____

_____

_____

_____

_____

345. Who is your ideal "you" now?

_____
_____
_____
_____
_____
_____
_____
_____
_____
_____
_____
_____
_____
_____
_____
_____
_____
_____
_____
_____
_____
_____
_____
_____
_____
_____
_____
_____
_____
_____
_____
_____
_____
_____

DATE : _____   SUBJECT : HERE & NOW

346. What makes you unique?

_____
_____
_____
_____
_____
_____
_____
_____
_____
_____
_____
_____
_____
_____
_____
_____
_____
_____
_____
_____
_____
_____
_____
_____
_____
_____
_____
_____
_____
_____

DATE : _____   SUBJECT : HERE & NOW

347. What is your favorite food, song, smell, activity and person right now?

_____
_____
_____
_____
_____
_____
_____
_____
_____
_____
_____
_____
_____
_____
_____
_____
_____
_____
_____
_____
_____
_____
_____
_____
_____
_____
_____
_____
_____
_____
_____

DATE : _____   SUBJECT : HERE & NOW

348. How would you describe the relationship you have with yourself?

_____

_____

_____

_____

_____

_____

_____

_____

_____

_____

_____

_____

_____

_____

_____

_____

_____

_____

_____

_____

_____

_____

_____

_____

_____

_____

_____

_____

_____

DATE : _____   SUBJECT : HERE & NOW

349. If you had only one year left to live, what would you spend it on?

_____
_____
_____
_____
_____
_____
_____
_____
_____
_____
_____
_____
_____
_____
_____
_____
_____
_____
_____
_____
_____
_____
_____
_____
_____
_____
_____
_____
_____
_____
_____
_____
_____
_____

DATE : _____   SUBJECT : HERE & NOW

350. Are you really doing what you want to do with your days? Do you like what you are doing with your life right now?

_____

_____

_____

_____

_____

_____

_____

_____

_____

_____

_____

_____

_____

_____

_____

_____

_____

_____

_____

_____

_____

_____

_____

_____

_____

_____

_____

_____

DATE : _____   SUBJECT : HERE & NOW

351. What are you thinking about right now? And why this specific thought?

_____

_____

_____

_____

_____

_____

_____

_____

_____

_____

_____

_____

_____

_____

_____

_____

_____

_____

_____

_____

_____

_____

_____

_____

_____

_____

_____

_____

DATE : _____   SUBJECT : HERE & NOW

352. Do you feel that you use your time in the best possible way? Why or why not?

_____
_____
_____
_____
_____
_____
_____
_____
_____
_____
_____
_____
_____
_____
_____
_____
_____
_____
_____
_____
_____
_____
_____
_____
_____
_____
_____
_____
_____
_____
_____

353. What are your last thoughts before going to sleep?

_____

_____

_____

_____

_____

_____

_____

_____

_____

_____

_____

_____

_____

_____

_____

_____

_____

_____

_____

_____

_____

_____

_____

_____

_____

_____

_____

_____

_____

_____

_____

_____

_____

354. Which talent or skill gives you the greatest sense of pride or satisfaction?

_____

_____

_____

_____

_____

_____

_____

_____

_____

_____

_____

_____

_____

_____

_____

_____

_____

_____

_____

_____

_____

_____

_____

_____

_____

_____

_____

_____

355. Is it difficult for you to be yourself? Why or why not?

_____

_____

_____

_____

_____

_____

_____

_____

_____

_____

_____

_____

_____

_____

_____

_____

_____

_____

_____

_____

_____

_____

_____

_____

_____

_____

_____

_____

_____

_____

_____

_____

356. What thoughts, beliefs or situations do you hold onto that are no longer helpful to you?

_____
_____
_____
_____
_____
_____
_____
_____
_____
_____
_____
_____
_____
_____
_____
_____
_____
_____
_____
_____
_____
_____
_____
_____
_____
_____
_____
_____

DATE : _____   SUBJECT : HERE & NOW

357. What have you learned lately that will lead you to a better future?

_____
_____
_____
_____
_____
_____
_____
_____
_____
_____
_____
_____
_____
_____
_____
_____
_____
_____
_____
_____
_____
_____
_____
_____
_____
_____
_____
_____
_____
_____
_____
_____
_____

358. What color would you choose to describe yourself? Why?

_____

_____

_____

_____

_____

_____

_____

_____

_____

_____

_____

_____

_____

_____

_____

_____

_____

_____

_____

_____

_____

_____

_____

_____

_____

_____

_____

_____

_____

_____

_____

359. What clothes are you most comfortable in?

DATE : _____   SUBJECT : HERE & NOW

360. What do you base your friendships on?

_____
_____
_____
_____
_____
_____
_____
_____
_____
_____
_____
_____
_____
_____
_____
_____
_____
_____
_____
_____
_____
_____
_____
_____
_____
_____
_____
_____
_____
_____
_____
_____
_____

DATE : _____   SUBJECT : HERE & NOW

361. What does "me time" look like to you?

_____
_____
_____
_____
_____
_____
_____
_____
_____
_____
_____
_____
_____
_____
_____
_____
_____
_____
_____
_____
_____
_____
_____
_____
_____
_____
_____
_____
_____
_____
_____
_____
_____
_____

DATE : _____   SUBJECT : HERE & NOW

362. Do you love the person you have become? Why or why not?

_____

_____

_____

_____

_____

_____

_____

_____

_____

_____

_____

_____

_____

_____

_____

_____

_____

_____

_____

_____

_____

_____

_____

_____

_____

_____

_____

_____

_____

_____

_____

_____

_____

363. What opportunities do you have now that you didn't have 1 year ago?

_____

_____

_____

_____

_____

_____

_____

_____

_____

_____

_____

_____

_____

_____

_____

_____

_____

_____

_____

_____

_____

_____

_____

_____

_____

_____

_____

_____

_____

_____

DATE : _____   SUBJECT : HERE & NOW

364. What have you learned during this year of introspection?

_____
_____
_____
_____
_____
_____
_____
_____
_____
_____
_____
_____
_____
_____
_____
_____
_____
_____
_____
_____
_____
_____
_____
_____
_____
_____
_____
_____
_____
_____
_____
_____

DATE : _____   SUBJECT : HERE & NOW

365. How do you see yourself and your life in one year's time?

_____

_____

_____

_____

_____

_____

_____

_____

_____

_____

_____

_____

_____

_____

_____

_____

_____

_____

_____

_____

_____

_____

_____

_____

_____

_____

_____

_____

_____

_____

_____

_____

www.ingramcontent.com/pod-product-compliance
Lightning Source LLC
Chambersburg PA
CBHW060448030426
42337CB00015B/1525